THE REALLY, REALL

STEP-BY-STEP
COMPUTER
BOOK 2

First published in 2004 by
Struik Publishers
(a division of New Holland Publishing (South Africa) (Pty) Ltd)
Cornelis Struik House
80 McKenzie Street
Cape Town 8001
South Africa

www.struik.co.za

New Holland Publishing is a member of Johnnic Communications Ltd

6 8 10 9 7 5

PUBLISHING MANAGER: Linda de Villiers
EDITOR: Joy Clack
DESIGNER: Beverley Dodd
ILLUSTRATOR: Cheryl Smith
PROOFREADER: Glynne Newlands
INDEXER: Brenda Brickman
SERIES CONCEPT: Gavin Hoole

Reproduction by Hirt & Carter Cape (Pty) Ltd
Printed and bound by Tien Wah Press (Pte) Ltd, Singapore

ISBN 10: 1 86872 899 4
ISBN 13: 978 1 86872 899 2

Log on to our photographic website **www.imagesofafrica.co.za** for an African experience

Contents

Read this before you start

 IF YOU'RE USING OTHER PROGRAMS OR VERSIONS:
This book is based on the Windows 98 operating system. If you're using a different version of Windows or one of the various Microsoft programs used in this book – or other brand name programs such as WordPerfect, AmiPro, Lotus, and so on – then you'll need to adapt where appropriate.

THE USER-FRIENDLY VISUAL SYSTEM

This book's user-friendly visual system makes it really, really, really easy for anyone to enjoy learning how to do things on a personal computer.

Colour-coded windows are used throughout the book so that you can see at a glance the *type* of information you're looking at:

- introductions and explanations in normal black text on a white background;

- step-by-step procedures in yellow boxes;

- hints and tips in blue boxes;

- very important notes and warnings in boxes with red borders;

- special exercises in green boxes.

Detailed procedures are supported where necessary by pictures of a PC screen or window to clarify what you'll see on your screen.

THIS IS A <u>WORK</u>BOOK:

Work through each chapter, from the beginning right through to the end.

Each chapter builds on the information covered in Book 1 and in earlier chapters of this book. The sequence has been specially designed to make it easy to increase your knowledge systematicall, so we **strongly recommend** that you don't skip any chapters, even if you think you already know that topic. Rather work through every chapter and every step-by-step procedure in the given sequence, starting right here with this important introductory chapter. You'll then have all the folders and files set up to do the various exercises as you come to them.

A few preliminaries

ABOUT USING THE MOUSE

Clicking means depressing the left-hand mouse button once and releasing it. This is usually done to open an item on a menu bar or to activate a button in a dialog box. It is also used on the Internet to activate a 'hyperlink' that will take you to a different Web page.

Double-clicking means depressing the left-hand mouse button twice in quick succession, then releasing it. This is usually done to open a program, folder or file.

Right-clicking means clicking the right-hand mouse button once and releasing it. This is usually done to open a menu.

Pointing means moving the mouse so that the pointer ⌖ touches the object on the screen to which you wish to 'point'.

Dragging means clicking and holding down the left-hand mouse button and moving the mouse to 'drag' or move or resize an item displayed on the screen, or to select a range of adjacent items.

CHANGING THE MOUSE PROPERTIES

Most people use the mouse exactly as it has been supplied. However, if you have any particular preferences, such as a faster clicking speed, you can change the mouse properties.

1. Click on **Start**, then **Settings**, then **Control Panel**.

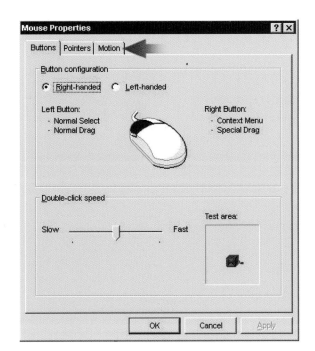

2. **Double-click** on the **Mouse** icon to open the **Mouse Properties** dialog box (a box that pops up on the screen for you to tell the computer which action to perform).

3. Click on each tab and select the options you require.

4. When done, click on **OK** to retain the changes, then click on the ☒ button of the **Control Panel** window to close it.

WHEN TO CLICK AND WHEN TO PRESS ENTER (OR 'RETURN')

Some people prefer to use the mouse, while others prefer the keyboard. Often there is a choice of which method to use when you want to tell the computer what action to perform. In some operations using the the mouse to click will be easier and quicker than pressing [Enter], while in other operations it's vice versa.

In a dialog box

In a dialog box there will usually be one button that is high-lighted with a shadow around it. (See picture – the **OK** button has a shadow around it to make it look 'raised'.)

This is the button that the computer has automatically assumed to be the one you want to activate. To activate it, simply press [Enter] on your keyboard. Alternatively, you can click on the shadowed button.

If you want to activate a *different* option – the **Cancel** button in the given example – then you need to **click** on that other button using the mouse. So, remember: if you press [Enter] on your keyboard, the button with the shadow around it will be the one that gets activated.

TIP:

Always read the info in a dialog box **before** clicking or pressing [Enter].

GETTING OUT OF TROUBLE

Some procedures you'll master immediately. With others you may need to re-read the instructions and try again. Be patient with yourself and make this a fun journey, and rest when you start to feel a bit tired.

Also, don't be afraid to experiment. If the wrong window pops up on your screen, you can usually get back to where you were by pressing the Esc key on your keyboard, or by using the mouse to click on the **Cancel** button in the unwanted open dialog box.

GETTING HELP

Help Boxes

To see what a button or icon means, place the pointer over it without clicking the mouse button and a little **Help Box** will pop up to give a brief explanation. This facility is available in all Microsoft programs.

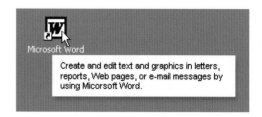

Using the F1 keyboard button

To get help when working in a particular program, such as **Word** or **Internet Explorer**:

> Press F1 to call up the **Help** menu for that particular program.

Getting more information on a particular item in view

To get a little more information about an item you see on your screen, use the **What's This?** help option. (This useful feature works for some Microsoft Office programs, but may not be available in other programs.)

> 1. Press Shift ⇧ + F1 and a question mark will appear alongside the pointer ⤵? .
>   (If you forget the shortcut, click on **Help** in the Menu Bar, then on **What's This?**.)
> 2. Click on the item on which you need extra information and an explanation box will pop up.
> 3. Press Esc to remove the ⤵? .

Okay, enough of the preliminaries. Let's get going with Chapter 1 – **Working with programs and windows**.

---

1 Working with programs and windows

The system that makes your computer function in response to the commands you give it is called the Operating System, and Windows 98 is the operating system covered in this book.

The 'software' you use to tell the computer to do certain things is comprised of 'programs', or 'applications'. There are programs for writing documents, sending and receiving electronic mail (e-mail), viewing Websites on the Internet, viewing pictures and listening to music, doing accounting, and more. A program, or application as it's often referred to, appears on your screen as a 'window'.

This chapter is about opening, closing and working with programs and their windows.

SWITCH ON YOUR COMPUTER

Switch on the computer and wait for it to **boot up** fully – that is, when you can see that it has finished loading the Desktop and Taskbar shortcut icons, and there is no machine noise other than the cooling fan.

CREATING A QUICK LAUNCH TOOLBAR TO OPEN PROGRAMS QUICKLY

This is a good time to set up your system so that you can load your favourite programs quickly. This will avoid time-consuming hunting around for the program name within the Start Menu each time you want to start a program.

A quick way to open any program – for example, Microsoft Word ('Word') – is to do so from a **Quick Launch Toolbar**. This allows you to get to a shortcut icon immediately without first having to get back to the Desktop. So let's first create such a toolbar.

1. **Right-click** on a blank area of the **Taskbar** (the grey strip to the right of the ⊞Start button) and a menu will pop up.

Taskbar

2. Point to **Toolbars**, and in the sub-menu that pops up click on **Quick Launch**. A new blank toolbar will appear on the Taskbar.

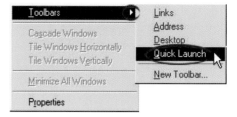

Cascading Menu

RIGHT-CLICKING TO CALL UP A MENU:

In almost any situation you can call up a menu by clicking on an area with the right-hand mouse button. The menu that pops up will relate to the area on which you are right-clicking. A small arrowhead icon ▶ on the right edge of a menu (see illustration above) means that the item expands to a further set of menu options in what is called a Cascading Menu.

ADDING A PROGRAM SHORTCUT TO THE QUICK LAUNCH TOOLBAR

As you'll be using Microsoft Word with this book, let's place a shortcut to **Word** onto the **Quick Launch Toolbar**. To do this, you first need to create a shortcut on the Desktop. This shortcut can then be copied to the Quick Launch Toolbar.

1. Click on 🏁Start and a menu will pop up.
2. Point to **Programs** (which has a little ▶ arrowhead next to it), and a sub-menu will appear after a moment or two.

3. Find the program called **W** **Microsoft Word**, and **right-click** on it.
   Another sub-menu will pop up.
4. Point to the words **Send To**, then click on **Desktop (create shortcut)**.
5. In the confirmation box that pops up click on **OK**.

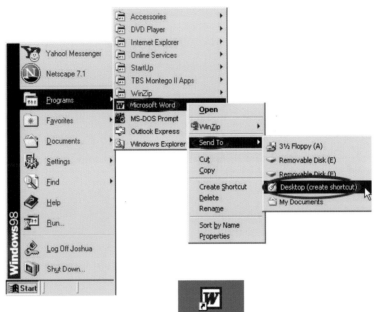

A shortcut icon will now appear on your Desktop.

To place a copy of this shortcut onto the Quick Launch Toolbar do the following:

6. Click on the shortcut icon and keep the mouse button depressed while you drag the pointer (and the icon) down onto the **Quick Launch Toolbar** (which is separated from the rest of the Taskbar by a thin, vertical, grey bar). This method is called drag-and-drop.
7. Keep holding down the left mouse button. A vertical black line will indicate where the icon will be positioned when you release the mouse button.

8. Release the mouse button and your shortcut to **Word** will now appear on the **Quick Launch Toolbar**. (It will usually remain on the Desktop as well.)

POSITIONING THE QUICK LAUNCH TOOLBAR

It's a good idea to position the Quick Launch Toolbar off the main Taskbar to leave space on the Taskbar for several buttons when you have a number of programs (applications) open at the same time. You can do this using the drag-and-drop method.

1. Point to the 'raised' vertical bar that shows where the Quick Launch Toolbar begins (just to the right of the ▓Start button).

2. Now click and hold down the mouse button. The pointer should change to a four-pointed cross. If it doesn't, try again and make sure you click on that narrow grey bar and not on the ▓Start button or the **W** **Word** icon.

3. Next, still holding down the mouse button, move your mouse upwards and left to move the ✛ to the far left edge of the Desktop, then release the mouse button. The Quick Launch Toolbar will reposition itself from the bottom Taskbar to the left-hand edge of your screen.

HIDING THE QUICK LAUNCH TOOLBAR

It's best to keep the Quick Launch Toolbar out of your way and available for quick use only when you need it.

1. **Right-click** on any blank area on the **Quick Launch Toolbar** and a menu will pop up.
2. If there is no tick alongside **Always on Top**, click on this item and the menu will close again. This will ensure that the toolbar is always visible on top of other windows that may be open.
3. **Right-click** again on the **Quick Launch Toolbar**.
4. Click on **Auto-Hide**. The toolbar will then disappear from view until you move the mouse pointer to the edge of the screen again, when the toolbar will reappear into view.

By doing steps 2 to 4 above, the Quick Launch Toolbar will be out of view when you don't need it. When you move the pointer to the far edge of the screen, it will again float into view and be visible on top of any window that may be open on your screen.

   If you have several programs open, you can now go straight to the Quick Launch Toolbar, which will pop up even if there is a program open on your screen and obscuring the Desktop.

IMPORTANT EXERCISE:

You're soon going to need to load **Windows Explorer** from a shortcut on the Quick Launch Toolbar, so now is a good time to practise creating another shortcut to this toolbar.

1. Follow the procedures given on pages 10–11 under the heading **ADDING A PROGRAM SHORTCUT TO THE QUICK LAUNCH TOOLBAR** to create a shortcut to the Desktop, then drag it from the Desktop to the Quick Launch Toolbar.

2. Instead of creating a shortcut for Microsoft Word, look for the program called **Windows Explorer** and create a shortcut for that program. (If it's already on your Desktop, that's great.)

3. Drag the shortcut onto the Quick Launch Toolbar, which will appear from hiding when you place your pointer at the left-hand or top edge of the screen, depending on where you placed it.

When you're done, your Quick Launch Toolbar should have two quick launch icons on it – one for Word and one for Windows Explorer.

LOADING PROGRAMS QUICKLY

Loading from the Quick Launch Toolbar

You can use the Quick Launch Toolbar to open any program for which you have added a shortcut to the Quick Launch Toolbar. To load a program:

1. Move the mouse pointer to the extreme edge of the screen where the Quick Launch Toolbar is hidden and the toolbar will float into view.

2. Click once on the **W** **Word** icon and Windows will open the word-processing program called Microsoft Word.

3. Repeat this procedure to click on the **Windows Explorer** icon to load Windows Explorer in the same way.

Windows Explorer (the last program you loaded) will appear on your screen and Word will be obscured behind it. Both programs will have their buttons down on the Taskbar, usually near the Start button.

Loading from a Desktop shortcut
When the Desktop is in view you can also load a program from a **Desktop** shortcut.

1. Hold down the ⌐Alt⌐ button, then press and release ⌐F4⌐ to close Windows Explorer.
2. Click on the ⌐×⌐ button in the top right corner to close Word.
3. With the Desktop now visible, find the **Internet Explorer** shortcut icon on the Desktop.

4. With your pointer over the shortcut icon, click the mouse button **twice** in **quick succession** (double-click). The program Internet Explorer will load and open on your Desktop.
5. When **Internet Explorer** has loaded, click on the ⌐×⌐ button in the top right corner to close it again.

PROGRAM CLOSING OPTIONS

METHOD 1	METHOD 2	METHOD 3	METHOD 4
With the program open and active, click on the ⌐×⌐ **Close** button at the top right corner of the title bar.	With the program open and active, press ⌐Alt⌐ + ⌐F4⌐ .	**Right-click** on the program's button on the Taskbar, then click on the **Close** menu option.	On the Menu Bar of the open and active program, click on **File**, then on **Exit**.

WORKING IN SEVERAL WINDOWS:

When two or more programs or files are loaded, usually only one will be visible on the Desktop, but they will all have their icons located on the Taskbar. The window that is visible on the screen will have its Taskbar icon depressed to show that this is the active window. If you click on the Taskbar button of a non-active window, that window will appear on the screen over the one that was previously visible. This is useful when you need to work in more than one program and switch back and forth between them. You simply click on the Taskbar button of the window you wish to view.

SWITCHING QUICKLY BETWEEN OPEN PROGRAMS OR FILES

A quicker method of switching between open programs, documents, pictures, and so on, is as follows:

1. Click on the [W] Word shortcut button on the Quick Launch Toolbar to load Word again.
2. Click on the [Windows Explorer icon] Windows Explorer shortcut button on the Quick Launch Toolbar to load Windows Explorer again.
3. With Word on the Taskbar and Windows Explorer visible on the screen, press [Alt] + [Tab] and Word will fill the screen.
4. Press [Alt] + [Tab] again to switch back (toggle) to Windows Explorer.

SWITCHING BETWEEN MORE THAN TWO WINDOWS:

To toggle through a menu of the open programs or files, keep the [Alt] key held down while pressing the [Tab] key once and then again. When you reach the one you want, release the [Alt] key and the program will be restored onto the screen.

The selected window will have a black border around it.

Document1 - Microsoft Word

DELETING A SHORTCUT

To delete a shortcut from either the Desktop or the Quick Launch Toolbar simply do this:

1. On the Desktop (or the Quick Launch Toolbar), **right-click** on the shortcut icon.
2. In the menu that pops up, click on **Delete**.
3. In the confirmation box that pops up, click on **OK**.

NOTE:

This will delete only the shortcut and not the program itself. If you ever need the shortcut again you can simply recreate it as described on pages 10–11.

DRAGGING DESKTOP SHORTCUT ICONS TO WHERE YOU WANT THEM

You can rearrange the icons on your Desktop to suit your needs.

Moving shortcut icons on the Desktop using drag-and-drop

1. **Right-click** on any blank area of the **Desktop**.
2. In the menu that pops up, point to **Arrange Icons** and make sure that **Auto Arrange** has **no** tick next to it. If it has a tick, click on **Auto Arrange** to remove the tick (this will enable you to manipulate the Desktop icons yourself). The menu will close.
3. **Click** on any **shortcut icon** and **hold down** the mouse button.
4. Move the pointer and the icon will move with it. This is called **dragging**.
5. **Release** the mouse button, and the shortcut icon will stay where you 'dropped' it.
6. Repeat the procedure with one of the other shortcut icons.

Arranging shortcut icons neatly on the Desktop
You can make the Desktop tidy again, with everything lined up neatly in columns and rows.

To line up the icons neatly:
Right-click on the Desktop, then click on **Line Up Icons** so that in their new positions they will be aligned in their respective rows. They will remain in the columns in which you dropped them.

To arrange them in sequence of name, type, size or date:
Right-click on the Desktop, then point to **Arrange Icons** and, in the menu that pops up, click on the option of your choice.

FINDING THINGS ON YOUR PC

Sometimes you may need to look for something on your computer, but have no idea where it is located. It may be a file, a folder, a shortcut, or even a program. Windows offers a quick search tool for finding things. In this exercise we'll look for a shortcut icon for a useful feature called **Show Desktop**, which allows you to get to the Desktop with one click instead of first having to minimize each open program in turn.

1. Click on , then **Find**, then **Files or Folders**. The **Find: All Files** dialog box will pop up.

2. In the **Named:** text window, type the words show desktop, make sure **[C:]** drive is showing in the **Look in:** window, then click on the **Find Now** button. Windows Explorer will open and display a list of files and folders containing the words **show** and **desktop**, including the shortcut file called **Show Desktop**.

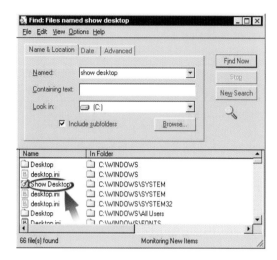

THREE TIPS FOR NARROWING A SEARCH:

1. Click the 🔽 **Look in:** arrow to get a drop-down menu; or

2. Click on **Browse** to browse for the folder in which you want to search; or

3. Click on the **Date** or the **Advanced** tab at the top to narrow the search.

Creating a shortcut from the Find dialog box

We'll now create a shortcut to Show Desktop, which we'll use in a later procedure.

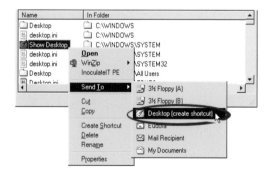

1. In the **Name** pane, click on the **Show Desktop** item to **select** it.

2. **Right-click** to get a menu, and point to **Send To**, then click on **Desktop (create shortcut)**.

3. In the box that pops up click on **OK** to create a shortcut icon on your Desktop.

4. Drag the shortcut icon to your **Quick Launch Toolbar** as explained on page 11.

Searching for unknown file names

When you're looking for a file, but can't remember its correct name, simply type what you think it is, or just a part of the name. Windows will find every item with that text in its name.

Searching all folders and subfolders

Make sure that the little white box next to **Include subfolders** has a tick in it. If not, click on it to give it a tick and, by default, Windows will search your entire **[C:]** drive.

Limiting the search to selected folders

If you know the file is located in a particular drive or directory, you can save time by telling Windows to limit the search to where you specify.

1. Click on the little arrow ▾ at the **Look in:** window to get the drop-down menu.
2. Select the directory or folder to be searched, for example **My Documents**.

Seeing more of the file name

Click on the little ▢ **Maximize** button (the middle one in the top right corner of the **Find** dialog box) and the box will maximize to full-screen size and display more of the file directory and name information.

Opening a file from the Find dialog box

Double-click on the file name, or click once and press Enter ↵ .

Closing the Find dialog box

With the **Find** dialog box open, click on the ⊠ button in the top right corner as usual, or press Alt + F4 .

MINIMIZING ALL PROGRAMS AT ONCE WITH ONE CLICK

If you have several programs running (i.e. you're 'multi-tasking'), you can use the Show Desktop shortcut button to view your Desktop with just one click, without having to minimize each program one by one to send them to the Taskbar.

Open several programs and/or documents, one after the other – **Word**, **Internet Explorer**, **Outlook Express**, and whatever other programs or files you want to load, so that your Desktop is obscured and there are several program/file buttons on the Taskbar.

Now try these two methods to get to the Desktop:

The long method:
1. Click on the ▣ **Minimize** button of the program that is filling your screen to send it to the Taskbar.
2. Repeat this to minimize the next program or file that is filling the screen.
3. Do it repeatedly until the Desktop is (finally) in view.

Restore the programs again:
Click on each shortcut button on the Taskbar to restore each of those items to the screen again, in turn. They will be one behind the other again. This will bring you back to where you were before using the long method.

The one-click method:
Move the pointer to where your Quick Launch Toolbar is hiding, and click once on the **Show Desktop** button on your Quick Launch Toolbar. All the programs will be sent to the Taskbar and your Desktop will be in full view.

TIP:
From now on you can use the **Show Desktop** shortcut whenever you need to get back to the Desktop quickly.

USING THE UNDERLINED LETTERS IN MENUS

You'll often find that one letter in each menu item is underlined. Look at the Menu Bar illustrated below and you'll see that the **F** in **File** is underlined. This indicates that you can either click on **File** to see the drop-down menu, or press [Alt] + [F] on your keyboard to give the computer a command to do the same task.

File Edit View Insert Format Tools Table Window Help

A typical Menu Bar

Try this:

1. Open Word.
2. Press [Alt] + [F] and the **File** drop-down menu will open.
3. Press [Esc] to remove the drop-down menu.
4. Now click **File** on the Menu Bar. The same thing happens: the **File** menu opens.

Underlined letters in drop-down menus

The underlined items in a **drop-down** menu indicate that you can access that menu item by pressing a letter on your keyboard as indicated by the underlining. The difference is that with a drop-down menu you don't need to use the [Alt] key as well.

Try this:

1. With Word still open, press [Alt] + [T] and the **Tools** drop-down menu will open.
2. Look for the item **Word Count** on that menu and notice that the **W** is underlined.
3. Press [W] on your keyboard (*without* also pressing [Alt]) and the **Word Count** box will open.
4. Press [Esc] to remove the box, or click on **Close**.

SHORTCUT BUTTONS ON DROP-DOWN MENUS:

Some menu items also have an icon button next to them, such as the A Font... item. This indicates that there is also a related **Font Color** button on the toolbar at the top of the program window (see illustration below), which can be clicked to change only the font colour.

THE GREYED-OUT ITEMS ON THE MENU:
In the shortcut menu example on the right you'll notice that some items, such as **Cut** and **Copy** are *greyed-out*. This means that those options are not available in that particular situation. (As you haven't selected any text there's nothing to *cut* or *copy*, and as you have not already copied anything, there is nothing on your clipboard to *paste*.) However, you could click on any available item that has its name in black, such as **Select All, Find, Replace**.

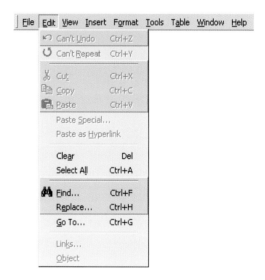

USING TOOLBAR SHORTCUTS

Toolbar buttons offer a quick and easy way to perform functions in most programs.

Example of a Standard Toolbar

Example of a Formatting Toolbar

NOTE: SOME TOOLBAR BUTTONS HAVE LIMITATIONS

Sometimes a toolbar button will perform a straightforward function without offering any options. For example, clicking on the 🖨 **Print** toolbar button will print one copy of a file in the printer's default (standard) settings. If you want to adjust some settings, such as the number of copies, printing selected pages only, print quality, and so on, then you need to press `Ctrl` + `P` or click on **File**, then **Print**, to bring up the **Print** dialog box to view the options.

Seeing what a particular toolbar button means

1. Move the mouse so that the **pointer** is over a **toolbar button**, but don't click.
2. Wait a second or so, and a little **ToolTip** label will appear below the button to tell you its function.

RESIZING A WINDOW

You can move a window around on your screen or in many cases actually make it wider or taller. This is very useful when you want to move one window out of the way to see something it's obscuring, but without closing it altogether, for example a Help window.

Try this:

Making a window wider

1. With any program open (for example Word), click once on the little 🗗 **Restore** button at the top right of the program window. The window will usually shrink in size.
2. Now slowly and carefully move your mouse so that the pointer hovers over the right-hand border of that window.

3. Move it ever so slightly and slowly until the pointer changes its shape to a small double-arrow (you may have to move it just a fraction to the left or right until it changes shape), then stop and hold it there.

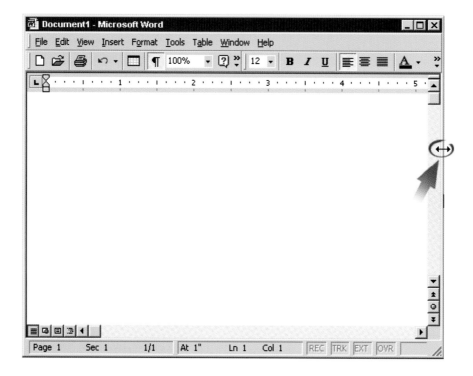

4. With the pointer in the double-arrow shape, left-click and hold down the mouse button.
5. Now drag the border a little to the left or right and notice how the window gets narrower or wider, according to the direction in which you dragged.
6. Release the mouse button and the window will stay at that new size.

You can do this on any border, and even on a corner. Try this:

Maintaining the proportion while resizing

1. Position the pointer on the **top left corner** of this window until it changes shape to a 45-degree angled double-arrow line.

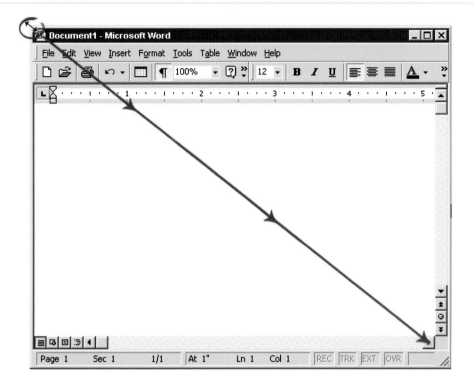

2. Click and hold down the left mouse button.
3. Now slowly drag the resizing arrows down **towards the bottom right-hand corner** of that window, and see how it shrinks the whole window proportionately.
4. Release the button.
5. Now do that again but drag the corner **outwards** so that the window becomes larger again. (Try doing this from other corners and sides too.)

Moving a window to a different position on the screen

Now let's try moving the whole window (without changing its size) to another position on your computer screen.

1. With the window in Restore size (not maximized), make sure it's resized to about half the screen size.
2. Click in the **blue border** at the top of that window and hold down the mouse button. (Your display settings may show the border as some other colour, and not blue, but the process is the same.)
3. Now carefully drag the pointer upwards and then let go. The whole window will move up accordingly.
4. Click again in the blue border and hold down the mouse button.
5. Drag the pointer to the left, and the whole window will move to the left.
6. Now click on the 🔳 **Maximize** button on the top right of that window to maximize the window back to its full size to fill your screen.

You can do this with almost any window to enable you to view several windows at the same time. This can be useful when you're reading instructions in one window, like a Help menu, and doing the suggested task in the main window: just drag the Help window out of the way. Or, if you are working in Word and researching information on the Internet at the same time, you can have both your Word program and your browser open at the same time and have each one reduced to fill one half of the screen, side by side or one above the other.

> **NOTE:**
> Only the window that has the dark border at the top is the active window. Windows with a grey border are inactive and the program won't respond until you click somewhere within that window or on the top title bar to reactivate the window. Note, too, that this moving and resizing of windows works only when the window is **not** in the maximized size, i.e. only when the 🔳 button is visible in the top right corner.

In the next chapter we'll cover some useful ways to organize your folders and files to make your tasks easier and more efficient.

2 Managing folders and files

Managing computer files is like managing files in a filing cabinet where you have labelled drawers containing labelled folders, with each folder containing individual documents or files with their own names. If you don't have an efficient filing system, you can waste a great deal of time hunting for things.

A program called Windows Explorer offers a good way to manage and work with all kinds of computer files. Note that this is WINDOWS Explorer, not INTERNET Explorer. The latter is used for exploring the Internet. Windows Explorer is the program for which you created a shortcut on the Quick Launch Toolbar in Chapter 1, and is used for exploring the contents of your computer.

So let's start by loading Windows Explorer now.

On the **Quick Launch Toolbar** that you created, click on the **Windows Explorer** shortcut button to open **Windows Explorer**. (If you don't have a Quick Launch Toolbar, refer to Chapter 1 – see page 9.)

Once Windows Explorer has loaded, a window will open similar to the one below.

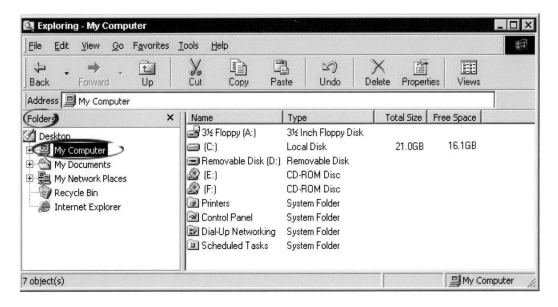

SETTING THE VIEW LAYOUT

If the layout on your screen is different from the illustration on page 27, you'll need to change the view layout as follows:

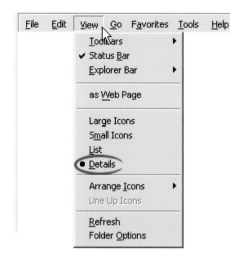

1. On the Windows Explorer Menu Bar click on **View** and make sure the **as Web Page** option has no black dot against it. If it does, click on it to remove the dot.

2. In the Menu Bar click on **View**, then on **Details** to set the view layout to show a detailed list of all your drives and folders. (It may already be set to this view layout.)

When you click on an item in the left-hand pane, you should see a detailed list of its files and folders in the right-hand pane. You may need to scroll down to see the rest of the folders.

TIP:

Notice that when **View, Details** is selected, more information about the files is shown – file, size, type and date modified. If the full file name is not visible in the first column of the right-hand pane, move the pointer up to the top of that pane and onto the little dividing line on the right of the **Name** heading, then click and drag the divider to the right to expose more of the first column.

The left-hand pane displays only the drives and folders, not the files. Files are always displayed in the right-hand pane and only once their **folder** in the left-hand pane has been clicked on to make it the 'active' folder.

TIP:

An item in the left-hand pane with a ⊞ next to it contains folders.

Click on the ⊞ icon to display the folders it contains, and the icon will change to ⊟.

Click on the ⊟ to close the folder again.

1. Click on the ⊞ icon next to the **My Documents** folder to display any subfolders. (See both panes.)

2. Now click on the **My Documents** folder itself to display its files as well as its folders.

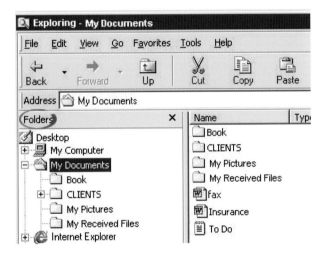

The left-hand **Folders** pane shows the various system folders on your computer, as well as the **My Documents** folder. The right-hand pane displays the contents of the item selected in the **Folders** pane, which will include any **files** and subfolders stored in the selected folder.

 Clicking on the ⊞ icon displays only the **folders** at the next level down, not the **files**. To display the **files** you need to click on the **folder** itself.

CREATING NEW FOLDERS

Just as a filing cabinet can have different filing drawers, each with its own filing sections, so too can your computer's filing system have different customized folders, each with its own sub-folders. This is a useful and logical way to manage your saved files for easy finding and opening.

Windows Explorer offers a very easy way to create a new folder, change a folder name, and move a folder elsewhere.

Creating a new folder

1. Load **Windows Explorer**. (If it's already loaded, click on [Exploring ...] on the Taskbar to make Windows Explorer visible on the screen.)
2. In the left-hand pane of Windows Explorer click on the **My Documents** folder to select it.
3. In the Menu Bar at the top, click on **File**, then point to **New** to open up the drop-down menu, and click on **Folder**.

A **New Folder** will be added in the My Documents folder, and will be listed in the right-hand pane. It will be highlighted (dark) and have a border around it so that you can give it a **folder name**.

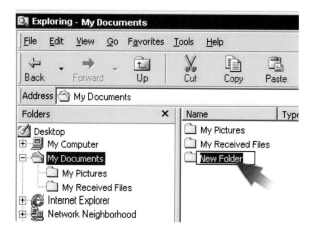

4. Type Computer Lessongs (yes, spelt that way) and press [Enter]. Your new folder will now bear that name.

Oops! We have a spelling mistake in that folder name. It should read Computer **Lessons**, not **Lessongs**. Let's fix that now.

RENAMING A FOLDER IN WINDOWS EXPLORER

1. **Right-click** on the **Computer Lessongs** folder to open a drop-down menu.
2. Read through the menu's items to see what actions are available.
3. Click on **Rena<u>m</u>e** and note how the folder now has a border around it, as when you first created and named it.

   Computer Lessongs
4. Retype the name in the folder so that it reads **Computer Lessons**.
5. Press ⏎ Enter , or click anywhere outside the folder name and the border will disappear; the folder will now have its new and correct name.
6. On the Menu Bar at the top, click on **<u>V</u>iew**, then **<u>R</u>efresh** to update the view in Windows Explorer. You should now see the new folder listed alphabetically under **My Documents** in the left-hand **Folders** pane.

OOPS!
Remember, if you 'mess up' you can press ⎋ Esc to get back to where you were and start again.

NOTE:
You can rename **files** as well as **folders** using this same procedure.

Don't attempt to rename any program-related (application) folders or files (e.g. in program-related folders, files with **.exe** behind the file name) or you will create major problems for yourself because the programs won't be able to operate. You can usually safely change the names of document folders and document (**.doc**) files, as well as picture files (**.jpg**, **.jpeg**, **.gif**, **.bmp**, **.tif**), Excel (**.xls**) files, PowerPoint (**.ppt** or **.pps**) files, and text (**.txt**) files.

CREATING SUBFOLDERS WITHIN FOLDERS

Let's set up some folders for you to use for your computer lessons and exercises.

1. In the left-hand pane, click on the folder you created earlier, named **Computer Lessons**, to select it.
2. On the Menu Bar click on **File**, point to **New**, and click on **Folder** to create a new folder within the **Computer Lessons** folder.
3. When the new folder appears type the name: Documents.
4. Press ⌷Enter⌷ and the new folder will now be named **Documents**.

TIP:

A new folder will always be situated within the folder selected. So, before you click on **File**, **New**, **Folder**, be sure that you first select the folder in which you want to create a new folder or subfolder.

---

5. Press ⌷Alt⌷ + ⌷F4⌷ to close Windows Explorer.
6. Click on the 🔍 **Windows Explorer** shortcut button to open **Windows Explorer** again.
7. Click on the ⊞ plus sign next to the **Computer Lessons** folder to open it.

You should now have the following folder structure:

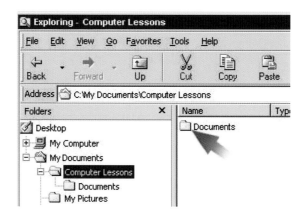

USING WINDOWS EXPLORER TO FIND AND OPEN FILES QUICKLY

You can open any file quickly, directly from Windows Explorer, without first having to load the applicable program. To demonstrate this, we'll first create and save a new file using Word.

Creating and saving a new file

1. Load **Word** from the shortcut you created.
2. With Word open, press Ctrl + N and a new document will open.
3. Type anything in the new document – just a few words or characters.
4. Now press Ctrl + S .

The **Save As** dialog box will open for you to specify where you want the document saved, and what file name you wish to give it.

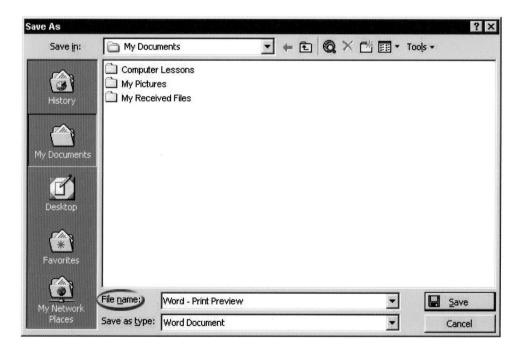

5. In the **File name:** window at the bottom, type: Word — Print Preview.
6. Click on **Save**, or press Enter , and the document will be saved in the
   My Documents folder with the file name **Word – Print Preview**.
7. Press Alt + F4 to close the document again.
8. If Word remains open, press Alt + F4 again to close Word.

1. In Windows Explorer, click on **My Documents** to display all its contents in the right-hand pane – the subfolders as well as the files – which will be listed alphabetically.

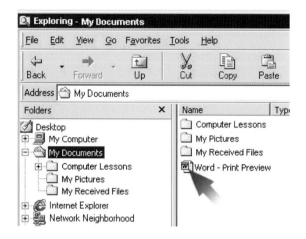

2. **Double-click** on the file **Word – Print Preview** and Windows will automatically load **Word** and display that document in the Word window. (Windows Explorer will be sent to the background with its button on the Taskbar.)

TIP:

You can open any file in this way and Windows will automatically load the appropriate program for viewing the file – for example Word for documents, Media Player for sound files, and so on. Some people open their files exclusively through Windows Explorer. It's also useful for easily seeing where you have stored your various files.

Try it a few times and see how you like using this quick method.

REARRANGING YOUR FOLDERS AND FILES FOR EFFICIENCY

As you create more files and folders on your PC, you may want to rearrange your filing system somewhat. To demonstrate how, we'll move the file **Word – Print Preview** from the **My Documents** folder to the subfolder called **Documents**.

1. In the **left-hand pane** of the open Windows Explorer click once on the folder named **My Documents** to display its contents in the **right-hand pane**, which should include the file named **Word – Print Preview**.

2. Now click on the ⊞ icon next to the folder named **Computer Lessons** to view its subfolders. The folder named **Documents** should now be visible.

3. In the right-hand pane click on the file named **Word – Print Preview** and hold down the mouse button while carefully moving the pointer into the left-hand pane and onto the folder named **Documents**, until that folder goes dark to indicate that it's been selected.

4. Now release the mouse button and the file **Word – Print Preview** will be relocated from the **My Documents** folder to the folder named **Documents**, which is a subfolder of **Computer Lessons**.

5. If you mess up and drop it into the wrong folder, click on **Edit** (on the **File** menu), then on **Undo Move**, and try again.

TIP:
You can use this same drag-and-drop method to move folders around, too.

REMINDER:
Items in the left-hand pane that have ⊞ next to them contain folders and files.
Folders *without* the ⊞ contain only files.

NOTE:
An alternative method for moving folders and files is to right-click on the item you want to move, and click on **Cut** on the drop-down menu to remove the item to the Clipboard. Then select the destination folder you want to move it to, and press Ctrl + V to paste the item into its new location.

SELECTING SEVERAL ITEMS AT ONCE

Here's an easy way to select several files at the same time. You can use it in many situations, for example:
- to select several files you wish to move or delete;
- to select and delete several e-mails from your e-mail IN folder.

There are two methods and each is applied according to the specific situation:

To select a range of adjacent items:	To select only some items:
1. Holding down the Shift key, click on the first item in the list, then on the last item you want to select. All items in between will automatically be selected as well.	1. Hold down the Ctrl key while clicking on each file you want to select.
2. Release the Shift key and perform the desired action (delete, copy, drag, etc.).	2. Release the Ctrl key and perform the desired action (delete, copy, drag, etc.).

DELETING FILES OR FOLDERS IN WINDOWS EXPLORER

When you no longer need a folder or a file you can simply delete it.

1. In Windows Explorer click on the folder named **Computer Lessons** that you created.
2. Press Del and in the confirmation box that pops up click on **OK**. The file and all its contents will be sent to the trash can (called the Recycle Bin).
3. Click on **View**, then on **Refresh** to see an updated Windows Explorer window with the folder no longer there.

To restore the folder for later use:
1. On the Menu Bar click on **Edit**, then on **Undo Delete**, and the folder will be restored as a subfolder of the My Documents folder.
2. Click on **View**, then on **Refresh** to see an updated Windows Explorer window with the folder restored in its position.

When you delete a **folder**, Windows will also delete all its contents. So before deleting a folder check what's inside it to be sure you're happy to delete all the folder contents along with the folder.

CREATING A USEFUL SHORTCUT TO NOTEPAD

Notepad is a useful item to have on your Quick Launch Toolbar. Whenever you need to make a quick note of something, perhaps an e-mail address, a comment off a Web page, or a shopping reminder, click on your Notepad shortcut and type your note, then save it. Here's how:

1. **Right-click** on any blank area of the Desktop and a menu will open.
2. Point to **New**, then click on **Text Document**, and a shortcut will appear on your Desktop ready to be named.
3. Type the file name Notes and press `Enter ↵`.
4. Now follow the procedure already explained in Chapter 1 to drag the shortcut onto your Quick Launch Toolbar.
5. Click on the shortcut to open your **Notes** text document.
6. Type anything into the document.
7. Press `Ctrl` + `F4` to close Notepad. It will ask you if you want to save the changes.
8. Press `Enter ↵` or click on the **Yes** button to save the changes.

In future, when you need to make a quick note, simply click on the shortcut to open that file, add your new notes (and delete any old notes you no longer need in the document), then close and save your Notes text document again.

In the following chapters you're going to make good use of this file management knowledge when you create and save documents, and open saved documents. You'll also learn more new and useful things you can do with Microsoft Word.

3 Working with documents in Word

In this chapter you'll be working with the word-processing program called Microsoft Word (Word) and learning how to work efficiently and professionally with documents. So, let's start.

Click on the [W] shortcut on your Quick Launch Toolbar to load **Microsoft Word**.

GETTING TO KNOW THE WORD WINDOW

The coloured Title and Document Bar

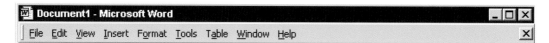

When a window is active its Title and Document Bar at the top of the Word window is darkened and the window will respond to your keyboard commands. When it's inactive the bar will be grey.

To make any inactive window active for use:
Click in the grey **Title and Document Bar**, or anywhere else in the window.

The Menu Bar

Each heading opens a door to a menu of items that can be selected by clicking on them.

1. Click on any menu heading to view its menu list.
2. Where you see ▶ next to an item, move the mouse pointer onto it to see a drop-down menu.

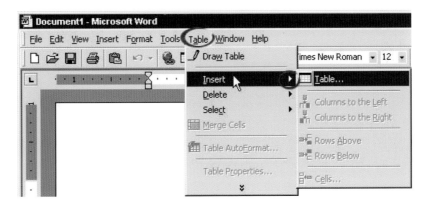

Menu with drop-down menu

The Toolbars

The buttons on a toolbar act as a quick way for you to give the computer commands, such as opening a new blank document or a saved document, printing a document, copying text, inserting a table, and so on.

TOOLBARS VERSUS MENUS:
Remember, a menu will usually offer more options than a toolbar button.

OPENING A NEW BLANK DOCUMENT

With the Windows operating system there are often several options available for doing the same task. Here are three different ways to open a new blank Word document. Try each one.

From the keyboard:

1. Press `Ctrl` + `N` and a new document will open.
2. Press `Alt` + `F4` to close the document again.

From the Standard Toolbar:

1. With Word still open, click on the **New Blank Document** button at the left end of the toolbar and a new document will open.

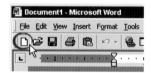

2. Press `Alt` + `F4` to close the document again.

From the Menu Bar:

1. With Word still open, click on File, then click on **New** and a new document will open. Some versions of Word may have a sub-menu on which you would select Blank Document.

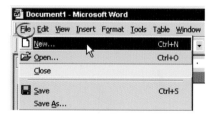

2. Press `Alt` + `F4` to close the document again.

Getting going with documents

We're now going to start working in documents, so with Word open start a new document using one of the methods described on page 40.

CUSTOMIZING THE PAGE SET-UP

You can change the size and layout of the page according to your particular needs – for example page size (A4, A5, legal, various envelope sizes), orientation (landscape or portrait), and so on.

1. On the **Menu Bar** (top left of the Word window), click on **File**, then **Page Setup**.
2. Note the various tabs at the top of the **Page Setup** dialog box.

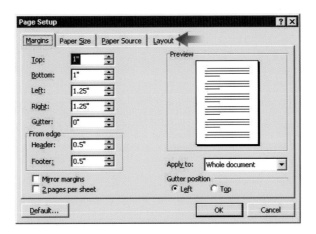

METRIC OR IMPERIAL?

To change your default measurement system click on **Tools, Options** and select the **General** tab. Change the **Measurement units:** to what you require.

On the **<u>Margins</u>** tab, the **<u>Top</u>:** margin has automatically been preselected by Word.

3. Type the number 2 and the existing measurement will be changed to 2.
4. Press 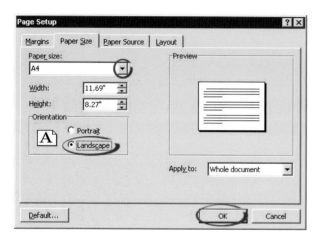 and the cursor will jump to the next little window (**<u>Bottom</u>:** margin).
5. Type the number 2 again and 2 will now appear in that window.
6. Repeat this process by pressing [Tab] again and changing the measurements for the left and right margins.
7. Note the other choices available lower down on that tab as well.
8. Click on the **Paper <u>S</u>ize** tab at the top to open another set of choices.

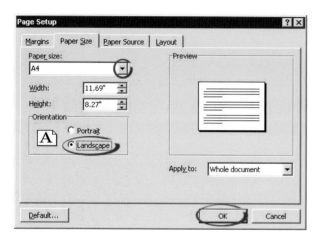

HINT:
Instead of using the mouse to move the cursor from one choice to another, and then clicking, it's often quicker to simply press the [Tab] key. This will automatically move the cursor to the next little window. This useful method can be used in any dialog box.

9. Click on the little black drop-down arrow ▾ next to the **Pape<u>r</u> size:** window.
10. Click on **A4**.
11. Under **Orientation**, click in the **Land<u>s</u>cape** white 'radio button' circle to select that option.
12. Click on **OK** (or press [Enter]) and your document will now display its new page setup.

ABOUT 'DEFAULTS':
Clicking on **OK** will affect the current document only. To change all future documents to new specifications and layout you would need to click on **<u>D</u>efault** (bottom left of the dialog box). So don't click on **<u>D</u>efault** unless you wish to affect all future documents as well.

SAVING A NEW DOCUMENT

There are several ways to save a new document. Here are three:

From the Menu Bar:	**From the Toolbar:**	**From the keyboard:**
Click on **File**, then **Save**.	Click on the 💾 **Save** button.	Press Ctrl + S .

The **Save As** dialog box will open for you to specify where you want the document saved, and what file name you wish to give it.

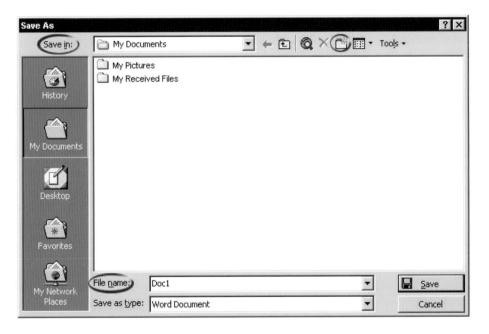

Saving to a new filing folder

By default, Word will offer to save your documents into the **My Documents** folder. Over time, however, this folder can become very cluttered with many different files all mixed up together in one folder. It's best to save and store your various documents and other files in an orderly system of folders, much like you would in a desk or filing cabinet. To do this you need to create new folders within the main My Documents folder. You've already learnt how to create a new folder in Windows Explorer, but here's how you do it while you are in the process of saving a new document in Word.

1. With a new document open, first use one of the three methods explained on page 43 to open the **Save As** dialog box.
2. Next, click on the [icon] **Create New Folder** icon in the dialog box.
3. In the **New Folder** dialog box that pops up, type the following in the **Name:** window: Computer Exercises. (This will be the name of the new **folder**, not the document.)

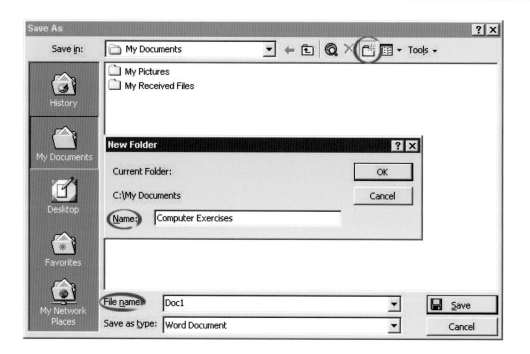

4. Click on **OK** in the **New Folder** dialog box and Windows will close the **New Folder** dialog box, leaving the **Save As** dialog box still open.

Your new folder's name will now appear in the **Save in:** window (which previously showed **My Documents**).

Windows will have selected the **File name** window for you to type in the name of your new document file.

5. Type the file name: Copy & Paste.
6. Click on **Save**, or press [Enter] and the document will be saved in the **Computer Exercises** folder with the file name **Copy & Paste**.
7. Keep the document open for the next exercise.

HINT:

When starting a new document, it's always a good idea to decide into which folder you want save it, and then to save it **before** you start working in it. From then on, you can do a quick-save regularly as you type, by simply pressing [Ctrl] + [S].
The document will then automatically be saved to the same folder with the same file name. If you continue to do frequent quick-saves you'll significantly reduce the risk of losing your work should the program or your computer system malfunction.

Saving an existing file as a new file name

When you wish to save a new version of a previously saved document, without losing the earlier version, you need to save it with a new file name. It's best to do this before you start editing the original saved document. This will ensure that you don't replace the old one with the new version. We'll use the existing file named **Copy & Paste** to demonstrate.

1. With your file still open, click on **File** in the Menu Bar, then on **Save As**. (Do **not** press [Ctrl] + [S].) The **Save As** dialog box will open with the current file name selected.
2. Type the following new file name: Toolbars, and the new name will overwrite the previous name in the dialog box.
3. Click on **Save** or press [Enter] and the document will be saved with its new file name. The earlier file, **Copy & Paste**, will still exist and be unchanged in the folder.
4. Press [Alt] + [F4] to close the document for the next exercise.

Remember, when you press ⌨Ctrl + ⌨S or click on the 🖫 **Save** button on the toolbar to re-save an *already saved* document, it will automatically be saved to its present folder and file name. If you wish to save an already saved document to a *new folder*, or with a *new file* name, you **must** use the **File, Save As** saving method so that the **Save As** dialog box will pop up to give you the saving options.

OPENING A RECENTLY USED DOCUMENT

There are several quick ways to find and open a document or file you've recently used. Windows keeps a record of these in at least two quick-find places.

Preparation:

1. In Windows Explorer open the file named **Word – Print Preview**.
2. Press ⌨Alt + ⌨F4 to close the document again.

Opening from the Word Menu Bar:

1. In Word, click on **File** and you will see a list of the last few documents used, in the sequence in which they were last open.
2. Click on the document name **Word – Print Preview** and it will open in Word, ready for you to start editing.

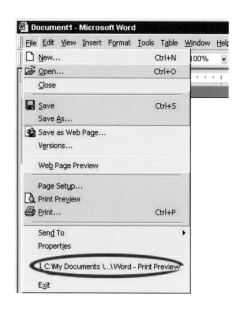

NOTE:
If you see little arrows ⌄ pointing downward at the bottom of a menu list, this means there are more items to view in the menu. To see the rest of the menu list, click on or point over the arrows to expand the menu.

Press **Alt** + **F4** to close the document for the next procedure.

Opening from the computer's **Start** **button:**

1. Click on **Start** at the bottom left of your screen.
2. Point to **Documents** and a list of recently opened files will appear.
3. Click on the document named **Word – Print Preview** and it will open in Word, ready for you to start editing.

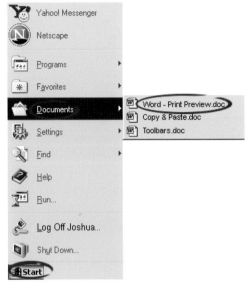

Recently opened Documents Menu

NOTE:

You can use this second method for opening any file, not just Word files, and Windows will automatically load the appropriate program needed for opening the file, whether it is a document file, a picture file or some other type of file.

IMPORTANT PREPARATORY TASK:

You'll need a four-page Word document to be able to work through the procedures that follow. Here's a quick way to create one: simply type a small section of text and then use the 'copy-and-paste' method to duplicate it over and over again until the document reaches four pages in length. So, here we go:

1. Open the document you saved as **Word – Print Preview**.
2. Type the first paragraph of this exercise box into the document.
3. At the end of the text you've typed, press **Enter** twice to create a new paragraph and a line space.
4. Press **Ctrl** + **A** to select all the text on the page you've typed (it will be highlighted in black).
5. On the formatting toolbar, click on the drop-down arrows to select a font style and size of your choice.

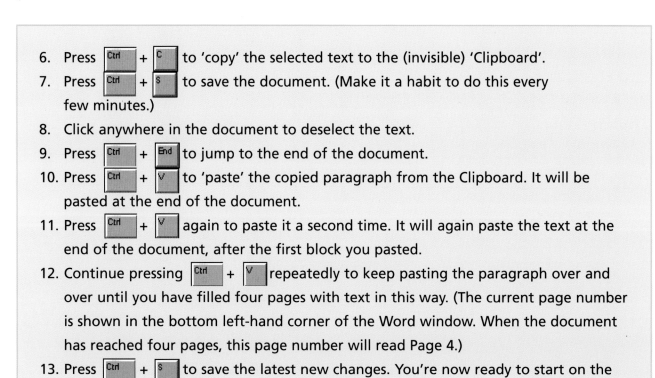

6. Press `Ctrl` + `C` to 'copy' the selected text to the (invisible) 'Clipboard'.

7. Press `Ctrl` + `S` to save the document. (Make it a habit to do this every few minutes.)

8. Click anywhere in the document to deselect the text.

9. Press `Ctrl` + `End` to jump to the end of the document.

10. Press `Ctrl` + `V` to 'paste' the copied paragraph from the Clipboard. It will be pasted at the end of the document.

11. Press `Ctrl` + `V` again to paste it a second time. It will again paste the text at the end of the document, after the first block you pasted.

12. Continue pressing `Ctrl` + `V` repeatedly to keep pasting the paragraph over and over until you have filled four pages with text in this way. (The current page number is shown in the bottom left-hand corner of the Word window. When the document has reached four pages, this page number will read Page 4.)

13. Press `Ctrl` + `S` to save the latest new changes. You're now ready to start on the sections that follow, using your four-page document.

A NOTE ON THE COPY-AND-PASTE METHOD:

You can also use this copy-and-paste procedure to copy items from one document to another and even from one program to another, such as from Word to your e-mail program. Once an item has been copied to the Clipboard, it remains available for immediate 'pasting' until it is superseded by a subsequent Copy action.

CHOOSING WHERE TO START A NEW PAGE

Sometimes it's desirable to end one page at a specific point and to continue on a new page even when the current page is not full. This is easy. You can do it while you are typing or once you've completed the whole document.

1. In the document **Word – Print Preview**, click where you wish to start a new page.
2. In the Menu Bar click on **<u>Insert</u>**, then **<u>Break</u>**, then **<u>P</u>age break**.

3. Click on **OK**, and Word will automatically start a fresh page within the same document. (The keyboard shortcut <kbd>Ctrl</kbd> + <kbd>Enter</kbd> will achieve the same effect.)

> **TIP:**
> The pages after a page break will continue with the same page setup as the previous pages. If you wish to change the page setup on subsequent pages (for example margins, orientation, columns) you need to select one of the **Section break types** listed in the **Break** dialog box. And to change the page setup for later pages, you'll need to insert a new **Section break** again.

VIEWING ENTIRE PAGES IN PRINT PREVIEW

Before printing a document you can preview what it will look like when printed.

1. Press ⎡Ctrl⎤ + ⎡Hom⎤ to go to the top of Page 1 in your document.

2. On the Word toolbar at the top, click on the 🔍 **Print Preview** button and the page will be reduced so that the entire page can be seen on the screen. (The thin blue border around the page indicates the selected page.)

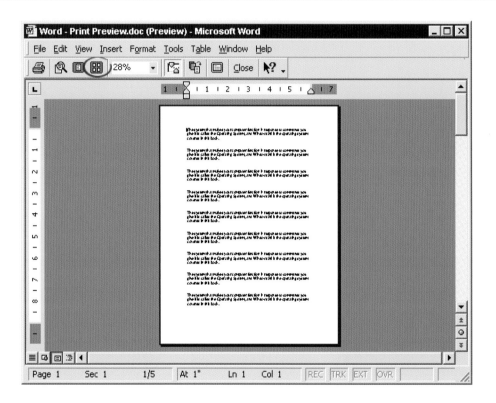

3. To view three pages alongside each other, click on the ⊞ **Multiple Pages** toolbar button and, in the little options frame that pops up, click on the **third frame** in the **top row**. (The selected page will have a thin blue border around it.)

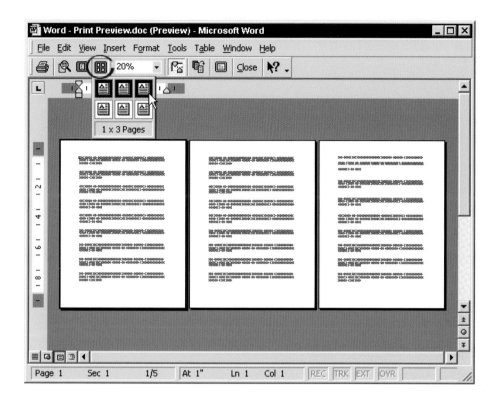

4. Now click on the ⊞ **Multiple Pages** toolbar button again, and in the little options frame that pops up click on the **third frame** in the **bottom row** so that up to six pages can be viewed at a time.

NOTE:

You can also view two pages alongside or above each other, or four pages, depending on which item you click on in the little frame of the **Multiple Pages** options. Try it.

Selecting a particular page in Print Preview

Click on the page you wish to select and that page will now show the thin blue border.

Magnifying the view in Print Preview

To zoom in from a reduced-size view to full size, do this:

1. Move the pointer onto the selected page and the pointer will change into a 🔍 magnifying glass icon.
2. Click once and the page will zoom out to 100% text size.
3. To return to the reduced view, click anywhere on the page again.

Viewing in Full Screen mode while in Print Preview

To see the biggest view of the full page in Print Preview mode:

1. Click on the ▣ **Full Screen** button on the toolbar.
2. To return to normal Print Preview mode, click on the **Close Full Screen** button.

WORKING WITH A DOCUMENT IN DIFFERENT SCREEN LAYOUTS

You can choose how you want to view your document on the screen while you're working in it. There are four basic views you can use:

Normal View 📄	This is the basic view for typing, editing and formatting text quickly. It does not show page boundaries, headers, footers, images, and so on.
Web Layout View 📄	This is used when you wish to see the document as it would appear as an Internet Web page. It's not usually used for general Word document viewing.
Print Layout View 📄	This is the best option for viewing your document with all its elements – headers, footers, margins, columns, images – as they would appear when the page is printed.
Outline View 📄	This shows the structure of the document and is useful for structuring longer documents into headings, subheadings and so on, but without page boundaries, headers, footers or graphics displayed.

There are two methods for changing the view:

From the Menu Bar:

In the Menu Bar, click on **View**, then click on the view you require. (Test each one to see the effect. The Menu Bar may have only three View options visible. Allow the menu to expand to full view.)

From the View Toolbar:

On the left of the bottom Scroll Bar in the Word window, click on the View button of your choice. Try each one now to see how it works.

TIP:

The best view for general work is the Print Layout View because you can see on screen everything that will appear on your printed document. However, some people prefer Normal View, so choose the one with which you are most comfortable.

Using Zoom to change the page view size

You can also change the view size of the document while you're working in it, to see it in a more appropriate size relative to the job you're doing.

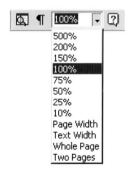

1. On the standard toolbar click on the **Zoom** arrow to open the drop-down menu of view sizes.
2. Click on the view size of your choice.

MOVING AROUND WITHIN A DOCUMENT

There are several ways of moving around in a document and it's a good idea to know them all.

Using the scroll bars

1. One line at a time:
On the vertical **Scroll Bar** on the right-hand side of the Word window, click on one of the arrows. The ▲ **top arrow** scrolls up one line, the ▼ **lower arrow** scrolls down one line. (If you hold down the mouse button the document will scroll continuously.)

2. A chunk of a page at a time:
Click in the grey area of the scroll bar, above or below the ▨ **Scroll Box** to scroll up or down respectively.

3. A full page at a time (in Page Width zoom size):
Click on the ⬍ **top** or ⬍ **bottom double-arrowhead** to scroll up or down a full page at a time.

4. Continuous scrolling:
Click on the ▨ **Scroll Box** and with the mouse button held down, drag the box up or down for a fast continuous scroll. When the box is right at the top of the scroll bar you will be at the top of the entire document, and vice versa.

Using the mouse wheel (if your mouse has one)

Roll the mouse wheel forwards to scroll up, and vice versa.

> **NOTE:**
> Some mouse models have other fancy options too, and the instructions are given with the packaging or accompanying manual.

Using the keyboard

1. Press ⌨`PgU` or ⌨`PgD` to move up or down in the document respectively.

Jumping to a specific page or section

1. Press ⌨`Ctrl` + ⌨`G` and the **Find and Replace** dialog box will pop up with the **Go To** tab and the **Next** button selected.

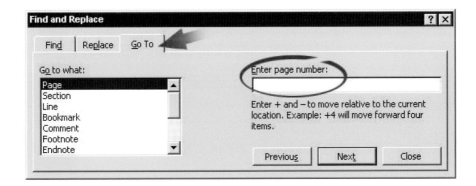

2. In the **Enter page number:** window, type the number of the page to which you want to go, or use one of the options mentioned below the **Enter page number:** window. The **Next** button will change to a **Go To** button.
3. Click on the **Go To** button.

NOTE:

As in most procedures, the keyboard shortcut is an alternative to using the Menu Bar. In this example, you would click on **Edit**, then **Go To** on the Menu Bar.

FINDING AND REPLACING SPECIFIC WORDS IN A DOCUMENT

Found that you've misspelt a word, or you need to replace a word or phrase throughout the document? It's easy. Word allows you to do an automatic search-and-replace, either word by word, or all in one click.

1. Press `Ctrl` + `G` and the **Find and Replace** dialog box will pop up with the **Go To** tab selected.
2. Click on the **Replace** tab.
3. In the **Find what:** window type the word you want to replace.
4. In the **Replace with:** window type the replacement word.
5. Click on the option of your choice given lower down: **Replace**, or **Replace All**, or **Find Next**.

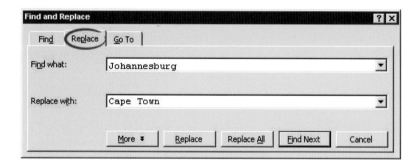

Narrowing your choice of text to be replaced

You can also specify that you want to replace only specific versions of the text, such as replacing **the Professor** (upper case 'P') with **the professor** (lower case 'p'), and leaving the word **Professor** with a capital 'P' wherever it appears in the document without the word 'the' before it.

In the **Find and Replace** dialog box click on the ⎡More ⏷⎤ **More** button for additional options.

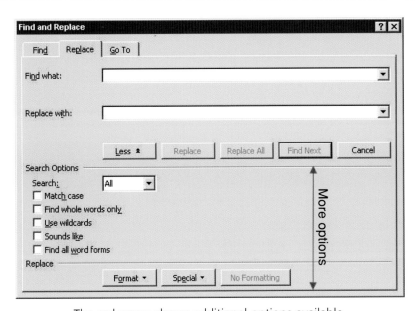

The red arrow shows additional options available

RESETTING FORMATTED TEXT TO YOUR NORMAL 'DEFAULT' FORMAT

Sometimes while you're typing you need to format some words or characters differently from the rest of the text, and then revert quickly to your normal 'default' font format. For example, perhaps you want to **type some words in bold** and some in ***bold italics***, and then continue in a normal font like this. Here's how:

1. To type in a different font style:
   • Press ⎡Ctrl⎤ + ⎡B⎤ to switch to **bold** font;
   • Press ⎡Ctrl⎤ + ⎡I⎤ to switch to *italics*;
   • Press ⎡Ctrl⎤ + ⎡U⎤ to switch to underlined text.
2. To return to the default font style and size, press ⎡Ctrl⎤ + ⎡Spacebar⎤.

Changing selected text to the default font format

You can, of course, also change the font format back to the default setting for all text in the entire document, or for a paragraph, sentence or word.

1. Select the text you would like to switch back to normal font format.
2. Press `Ctrl` + `Spacebar` and the selected text will reset itself back to 'normal' formatting.

MOVING TEXT TO A DIFFERENT POSITION

There are two popular ways to move text from one part of a document to another: the cut-and-paste method, and the drag-and-drop method.

Cut-and-paste method:

1. Type the following two sentences in a Word document, and press `Enter` twice to separate the two sentences with a paragraph and a line break so that they are two distinctly separate paragraphs.

   This is a useful trick to know.

   Cut and paste is a useful way to move large chunks of text from one place to another — even to another document or program.

2. Press `Enter` again after the second paragraph, to create a line space after paragraph 2 as well.
3. Select the second paragraph you've just typed. (Double-click in the left margin next to the sentence and it will be highlighted in black.) See below.

   This is a useful trick to know.
   ¶
   Cut and paste is a useful way to move large chunks of text from one place to another — even to another document or program.

4. Press `Ctrl` + `X` to cut out the selected text; this will copy it to the Clipboard.
5. Click at the beginning of remaining sentence: `'This is a useful trick to know.'`
6. Press `Ctrl` + `V` to paste the deleted paragraph in its new position.

Your two sentences will now appear as follows:

```
Cut and paste is a useful way to move large chunks of text from
one place to another — even to another document or program.
This is a useful trick to know.
```

Drag-and-drop method:
1. Click at the start of the first sentence and, holding the mouse button down, drag the pointer to the end of that sentence to select it. Release the mouse button.
2. Move the pointer onto the selected text, click and keep the mouse button pressed down, and drag the pointer to the end of the sentence: `'This is a useful trick to know'`.

```
Cut and paste is a useful way to move large chunks of text from
one place to another — even to another document or program.This
is a useful trick to know.
```

3. Release the mouse button and the text will be moved to its new position (see below).

```
This is a useful trick to know.Cut and paste is a useful way to
move large chunks of text from one place to another — even to
another document or program.
```

FORMATTING BULLET POINTS AND NUMBERED PARAGRAPHS

In addition to using the standard bullet points and numbers, you can play around and set the formatting according to your needs.

Setting the bullet indents

1. On the Menu Bar click on **F<u>o</u>rmat**, then **Bullets and <u>N</u>umbering**, and the **Bullets and Numbering** dialog box will open.
2. Click on the **<u>B</u>ulleted** tab and click on a bullet style of your choice from the list of examples shown.

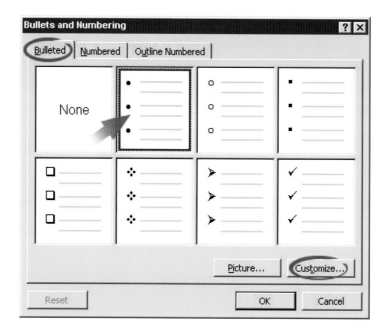

3. Next, click on **Cus<u>t</u>omize** to open the **Customize Bulleted List** dialog box.

4. In the **Bullet position** section select the number in the **Indent _a_t:** window and type 0 cm in its place.

5. In the **Text position** section select the number in the **_I_ndent at:** window and type 0.63 cm in its place.

6. Click on **OK** or press ⌷Enter↵⌷ .

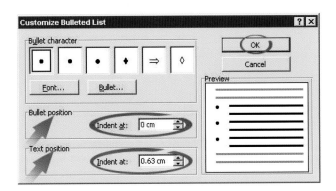

7. Type a few words, press ⌷Enter↵⌷ to create the next bulleted line, and type more text.

8. Press ⌷Enter↵⌷ again to create the next bulleted line and type more text, and so on.

For indents for numbered paragraphs, use the procedure given above using the **Numbered** tab.

Using multi-level bullets or numbers
You can easily create different numbering or bullet styles at various levels of itemized text.

Click on the **O_u_tline Numbered** tab and follow a similar procedure as described above to set the styles and indents you require.

To create multi-level bullets or numbering in a document:

1. Click on the ▤ **Increase Indent** button on the Word toolbar, and the line will shift to the right and the bullet/number will change appropriately.

2. Click the button again to create a further indent and level of bullet or numbering.

3. To return to the first level number format and indent, click the ▤ **Decrease Indent** button once or twice, as necessary.

CREATING HEADERS AND FOOTERS THROUGHOUT A DOCUMENT

Word lets you have the same header or footer on every page throughout your document, without your having to type it on every page. And you can format it independently of the main document, for example giving it a smaller font, a different colour, and so on.

1. Open the document you saved as **Word – Print Preview**.
2. In the Word Menu Bar, click on **View**, then **Header and Footer**. The **Header and Footer** dialog box will open with the **Header** window open for typing.
3. Type the following: Word — Print Preview — Page and then press Spacebar .
4. Click on the ⊞ **Insert Page Number** button in the dialog box, and the page number will appear in the header.

5. Click on the **Switch Between Header and Footer** button in the dialog box, and the **Footer** window will open for typing.
6. Click on the **Insert Date** button and press the Spacebar.
7. Click on the ◷ **Insert Time** button.
8. Click on the **Page Setup** button and click in the check box for **Different first page** to omit the header and footer text from the first page and have it appear only from page 2 onwards.

NOTE:

The Header and Footer **Page Setup** dialog box allows you to set up your headers and footers according to your preferences. Mastering the Header and Footer process might require some experimentation so that you can see the effects of the various options.

WORKING WITH TABS

A tab stop is a position that is set for placing and aligning text on a page in Word.

Default tab settings
Word has its own default settings for tab stops, typically every half inch or centimetre. The ruler at the top of the document window shows where the default tab settings are.

Default tab settings on the ruler

RULER NOT VISIBLE?

On the Menu Bar, click on **View**, then on **Ruler**, and the ruler will become visible.

METRIC OR IMPERIAL?

To change your default measurement system click on **Tools**, **Options** and select the **General** tab. Change the **Measurement units:** to what you require.

Changing the settings for a particular document
You will find the tab button options on the left-hand side of the horizontal ruler at the top of your Word window.

Click the little tab button to bring up the next option. Repeat to toggle to the next option. The options are explained below.

L Left Tab	All text aligns flush left and extends to the right from the left tab stop.
⊥ Centre Tab	Text is centred on the page with the tab being the centre point.
⊿ Right Tab	Text extends to the left from the right tab stop.
⊥• Decimal Tab	Text before the decimal tab extends to the left and text after the decimal point extends to the right.

Example:

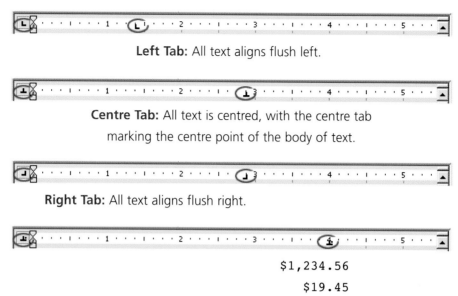

Left Tab: All text aligns flush left.

Centre Tab: All text is centred, with the centre tab marking the centre point of the body of text.

Right Tab: All text aligns flush right.

$1,234.56

$19.45

Decimal Tab: Text jumps to the tab stop and will show to the left of the tab stop until the full stop or decimal is typed. Subsequent text will then show to the right of the tab stop.

For users of Word 2000 or later versions

If you are using Word 2000 or later versions you will also have some extra options:

▯ Bar Tab	Does not affect the flow of the text, but allows you to place a vertical line in your document where this tab stop is set.
▽ First Line	Indents the first line of each new paragraph.
▢ Hanging Indent	Indents each line of a paragraph except for the first line.

Bar Tab: Inserts a vertical line at the tab point that doesn't affect text flow but simply inserts a non-printing guideline on the screen.

First Line Indent: First line of each new paragraph is indented to a specified position on the horizontal ruler.

Hanging Indent: First line of each paragraph begins at the margin. Subsequent lines are indented to a specified position on the horizontal ruler.

SWITCHING BETWEEN OVERWRITE AND INSERT MODES

When you need to insert text (letters or words) you can choose how you want the insertion to be added to your existing sentence:

- It can overwrite (delete) the existing characters after the insertion point (**Overwrite** mode); or
- It can be inserted without deleting the characters after it (**Insert** mode).

Overwrite mode:

Press the  key once to change to **Overwrite** mode, and the letters **OVR** will appear in the Word Status Bar at the bottom of the Word window.

Insert mode:

Press  again to switch back to **Insert** mode, and the letters **OVR** will disappear.

REC TRK EXT OVR 🔲	REC TRK EXT OVR 🔲
Overwrite mode	Insert mode

SEEING THE DOCUMENT'S FORMATTING STRUCTURE

When formatting a document it's often useful to see how you have created line breaks, how many spaces you've left between characters, words or paragraphs, or exactly where the tabs are, and so on. This can help you to maintain uniformity of layout throughout the document. The most frequently occurring marks are these:

¶   Paragraph break;

··¤   Character spaces;

→   Tab space.

1. Open the four-page document you created, the one named **Word – Print Preview**.
2. On the Word Standard Toolbar at the top, click on the ¶ **Show/Hide** button and notice all the formatting marks scattered throughout the document.

Show formatting marks

3. To hide the formatting marks, click on the ¶ **Show/Hide** button again.

In the next chapter you'll learn some useful techniques for creating letterheads, forms and other specialized documents.

4 Creating fancy documents in Word

Microsoft Word offers some useful and easy methods for creating special documents such as forms, letterheads, CVs, newsletters, and the like. These include:

Templates   – formats that are preset by Word (or created by you in Word) as the basis for creating specific kinds of documents;

Wizards   – computerized expert systems that guide you through the creating process by asking you what you want to do, as you go along, and giving you options from which to choose;

Tables   – structured boxes of rows and columns for aligning text in columns and rows, and for creating your own forms;

Columns   – divisions within a page that allow text to flow into two or more columns on the same page.

Using tables for columns, letterheads, forms

A very useful way of creating professional documents, forms or schedules, and aligning text in columns, is by inserting a table.

INSERTING A MULTI-COLUMN TABLE

1. On the Word Standard Toolbar click on the ⊞ **Insert Table** button.

2. Click in the fourth square in the first row to insert a four-column table of one row.

3. Press `Ctrl` + `S` to save your new document in the **Documents** folder, and give it the file name Tables.

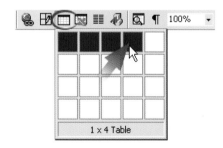

FOR MORE ROWS OR COLUMNS:

From the **Insert Table** button you can insert a table up to five columns wide and four rows deep. To have more columns you should rather click on the Menu Bar's **Table**, then **Insert**, then **Table**, and use the options available. Alternatively, you can add more columns later, but it can sometimes be a bit tricky fitting the extra columns into the page width. However, adding extra rows later is easy (see page 70).

SELECTING A CELL AND TYPING IN IT

Each 'box' in a table is called a cell. When the table is inserted, the cursor will automatically be positioned in the first cell (the first row in the first column). You can immediately start typing in this cell.

1. Type this into the first cell: 21 March
2. Press [Tab] to move to the second cell, and type this: Housekeeping
3. Press [Tab] again to move to the third cell, and type this: $120.00
4. Press [Tab] again to move to the fourth and last cell, and type this: Food
5. Press [Tab] again and Word will create a new row (Word always does this).
6. Press [Tab] again to move to the second cell in the second row, and type this: Entertainment
7. Press [Tab] again to move to the third cell in the second row, and type this: 85.00
8. Press [Tab] again to move to the fourth cell in the second row, and type this: Movies

Your table should look like this:

21 March	Housekeeping	$120.00	Food
	Entertainment	85.00	Movies

EDITING TEXT WITHIN A CELL

To edit text within a cell it is not necessary to select the whole cell.

Click in the text at the place you wish to edit the text, just as you would do if you were editing text that was not in a table.

SELECTING AND FORMATTING A WHOLE CELL

1. Move the pointer just to the **right** of the left border of the cell containing the text 21 March, so that the pointer shape changes to a right-pointing black arrow.

2. Click to select the cell.
3. Press Ctrl + B to change the text to **bold** font.
4. Move the pointer and click anywhere to deselect the cell.

PREPARATORY EXERCISE:

To prepare for the next few procedures, first add a few more rows to your table: hold down the Tab key and let the cursor run through the table, cell by cell, adding extra rows at the end as it goes. Note that with this method the additional rows are added at the end of the table.

SELECTING A WHOLE ROW

1. Move the pointer to the left margin just outside the table, and opposite the third row. The pointer will change to a ⟋ **right-diagonal arrow**.
2. Click and the whole row will be selected and highlighted.

21 March☼	Housekeeping ☼	$120.00 ☼	Food ↵
☼	Entertainment ☼	85.00 ☼	Movies ↵
✹	✹	✹	✹

You can now format this whole row in any way you wish, but for the purpose of demonstrating a later procedure, we'll format it by adding a shaded background.

FORMATTING A WHOLE ROW WITH BACKGROUND SHADING

1. With the row selected, on the Menu Bar click on **F̲ormat**, then **Borders and Shading** and a dialog box will open.
2. Click on the **Shading** tab.

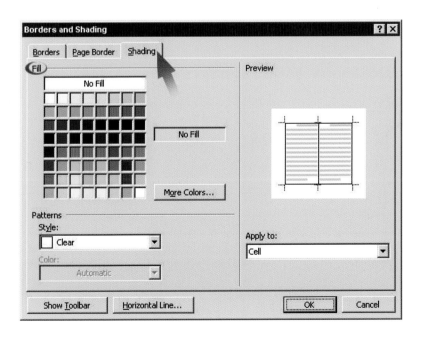

3. In the **Fill** section click on a pale colour of your choice. Notice the various other options for later investigation.
4. Click on **OK** or press Enter ↵ . The row will now have a shaded background.

SELECTING A WHOLE COLUMN

1. Move the pointer to the top of the third column containing costs in dollars, close to the top border so that the pointer changes shape to a ↓ black arrow.
2. Click to select the whole column. It will become highlighted and ready for formatting, changing alignment, and so on.

SELECTING MULTIPLE COLUMNS OR ROWS

You can also select several columns or rows provided they are adjacent to each other.

Selecting adjacent rows:
1. Select a row as explained earlier.
2. Holding down the mouse button, drag the pointer upwards or downwards to select the adjacent row/s.

Selecting adjacent columns:
1. Select a column as explained earlier.
2. Holding down the mouse button, drag the pointer left or right to select the adjacent column/s.

ADDING EXTRA ROWS ANYWHERE IN THE TABLE

If you were simply to hold down the ⌨ Tab key as before, the cursor would run through the table cell by cell and start adding rows only at the end. They would all follow the formatting of the row before. However, we want to add a row at a specific place, just before the shaded row.

1. Move the pointer to the left-hand margin outside the table, next to the row just **above** the shaded row, and click to select it as in the previous procedure.
2. Click on the ⊟ **Insert Rows** button on the Word toolbar and a row will be added just below the selected row.
3. Click the button again to add another row at the same place, and continue like this until you have added as many rows as you need.

Notice how the rows are added above the shaded row and 'push' the shaded row further down the table to make space for the additional rows.

> **NOTE:**
>
> All the additional rows take on the same formatting properties as the previous row. So if you were to select the shaded row and then start inserting rows, the new rows would likewise all be shaded.

CREATING TAB INDENTS WITHIN A TABLE

Because pressing the [Tab] key moves the cursor to the next cell, this method cannot be used for inserting tab indents within a cell. To add tab indents, simply do this:

> Press [Ctrl] + [Tab] and Word will create a tab indent within the cell, according to the size of the tab indents you have in your Tab settings.

RESIZING A COLUMN OR ROW BY DRAGGING ITS BORDER LINE

To make a column narrower or wider, you can drag it like this:

1. Move the pointer onto the vertical border line you wish to move, and the pointer will change shape to ←‖→ a pair of resizing arrows.
2. Click and hold down the mouse button as you drag the vertical dotted line to the left or right.
3. When the dotted line is where you want the column border line to be, release the mouse button. The column border will be moved to that point.

To resize a row, simply apply this same procedure to the row you want to adjust.

> **NOTE:**
>
> You can also make just one cell wider or narrower, without affecting cells in other rows. Simply select the **cell** and move one of its vertical borders using the same procedure as above. This does not work for horizontal borders.

SPECIFYING THE SIZE OF CELLS, COLUMNS AND ROWS

You can also use the Menu Bar to specify the size of cells, columns or rows.

1. Click anywhere in the table to select it.
2. In the Menu Bar click on **Table**, then on **Table Properties**.
3. Click on the various tabs to select the items you wish to change.
4. Click on **OK** or press ⌷Enter↵⌷.

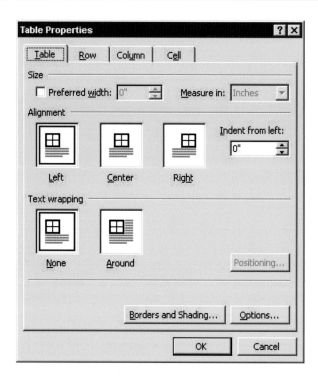

NOTE:

The **Alignment** option refers to the **table**, not the text, i.e. whether the table must be centred on the page, and so on.

ADJUSTING COLUMNS AND ROWS TO FIT THE CONTENTS OR THE PAGE WIDTH

If you're not sure how wide the columns should be, you can let Word adjust them for you. If you wish, you can modify them later by dragging their borders as described on page 71.

1. Move the pointer to the top of any column, close to the top border so that the pointer changes shape to a ↓ black arrow.
2. Click and hold down the mouse button to select that column.
3. With the button still held down, move the pointer sideways to select the next column as well.
4. Release the mouse button, and you will have two selected columns.
5. In the Menu Bar click on **Table**, then on **AutoFit** and click on the item you wish to use. Note how Word adjusts the sizes of the columns according to your selection.

ALIGNING TEXT IN DIFFERENT CELLS OR COLUMNS

Note that by default all the text in the table is left-aligned. This doesn't look good for columns containing numbers; numbers look best when they are right-aligned.

1. Click in a cell (or above a column) to select it.
2. To centre the contents, press `Ctrl` + `E` .
3. To right-align the contents, press `Ctrl` + `R` .
4. To left-align the contents, press `Ctrl` + `L` .
5. To justify the contents, press `Ctrl` + `J` .

DELETING THE CONTENTS OF A CELL

Select the cell as explained earlier, and press `Del` .

DELETING A WHOLE ROW, NOT JUST THE CONTENTS

Select the row as explained earlier, and press `Ctrl` + `X` or click on the Standard Toolbar's ✂ **Cut** button.

DELETING A WHOLE COLUMN, NOT JUST THE CONTENTS

Select the column as already explained, then press `Ctrl` + `X` or click on the toolbar's ✂ **Cut** button.

DELETING A CELL IN A ROW USING MERGING

Sometimes it's necessary to delete one or more cells in a row without deleting the whole row. This is called merging – merging two or more cells into one. This is particularly useful when designing forms, letterheads, and so on.

1. Select the two or more adjacent cells you want to merge into one.
2. Click on **Table**, then on **Merge Cells** and the cells will merge into one cell.

REMOVING TABLE BORDERS

Often you may not want to have border lines around or within a table. It's easy to remove these.

1. Click anywhere in the table to select it.
2. In the Menu Bar, click on **Table**, point to **Select**, and click on **Table** to select the entire table.
3. On the Formatting Toolbar click on the ▾ drop-down arrow next to the ▦ **Outline Border** button to open the box of border options.

4. Click on the ▦ **No Border** button.
5. Click anywhere to deselect the table, which will now have no borders at all although you may still see the grey non-printing gridlines on your screen.

SEEING OR HIDING THE NON-PRINTING BORDERS SHOWN ON THE SCREEN

Although you may have removed the border lines in the table, you will possibly still see grey borders around each cell on your screen. These are called gridlines and they are there to show you where each cell begins and ends. If you print the document, these gridlines will not be printed. Sometimes it is useful to remove the gridlines from view on the screen so that you can see the effect with no lines at all. But often it's best to have them in view while you are working in a table. Here's how to hide them:

Hiding Gridlines:
In the Menu Bar, click on **T̲able**, then on **Hide G̲ridlines**.

Showing Gridlines:
In the Menu Bar, click on **T̲able**, then on **Show G̲ridlines**.

INSERTING BORDER LINES SELECTIVELY

You can also add a border line only on certain borders of a cell or a table, for example only a bottom border of a cell or row, or an outside border around a column but not around the rest of the table.

1. First select the whole table and remove all borders as explained on page 74. This will make it easier to work only with the cells, columns or rows that you want to format with borders.
2. Select the cell, row or column you want to format.
3. On the Formatting Toolbar click on the ▾ drop-down arrow next to the ▦ **Outline Border** button to open the box of options.
4. Click on the button that depicts the kind of border you want for your selected cell/s.
5. Click anywhere to deselect the cell/s.

CONVERTING EXISTING TEXT INTO A TABLE

Sometimes you've already typed some text and think it would look better or be easier to format into different sections if it were in table form. Here's how:

1. Select the text you wish to convert to a table.
2. On the Menu Bar click on **Table**, then on **Convert**, then **Text to Table** and the **Convert Text to Table** dialog box will open.

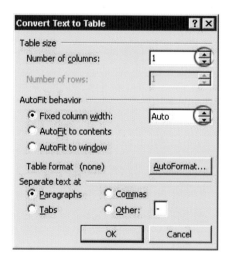

3. Use the little ⬍ up or down arrows to select how many columns you require in your table, and how you require the **AutoFit** to apply.

4. Next, you'll need to decide how you wish the text to be separated. This will affect how Word creates the rows. If you select wrongly, you may end up with far too many rows, with bits of text separated into different cells because of how you've chosen to separate it – by paragraph breaks, tab breaks, commas, and so on.

HINT:

If you don't like the way it looks the first time, simply click on the ↺ **Undo** button on the Word toolbar and you'll get back to where you were before converting **Text to Table**. You can then try again. Sometimes you may need to merge some of the cells after you've converted text to a table.

CONVERTING A TABLE INTO ORDINARY TEXT

You can also convert an existing table into ordinary text.

1. Click anywhere in the table to select it.

2. On the Menu Bar click on **Table**, then on **Convert**, then **Table to Text** and the **Convert Table to Text** dialog box will open.

3. Click on the appropriate item to indicate how you want Word to separate the text once it's no longer in a table. Experiment and use ↺ **Undo** until you get close to the layout you want, then format the text how you want it.

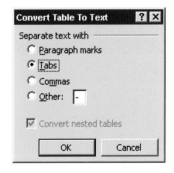

You may need to move some of the text around to get everything to look right, but this conversion process beats selecting each item and doing a cut-and-paste to get it out of the table.

USEFUL EXERCISE:

Using your knowledge regarding tables, create your own letterhead like the example given below. Follow these step-by-step guidelines:

1. Open a new blank document in Word.
2. Save the document in the folder called **Computer Exercises**, and give it the file name **Letterhead**.
3. Start by inserting a three-column, two-row table at the top of your new blank document called **Letterhead**.
4. Add text to the cells as shown in the example below.

Letterhead Name		
		P O Box 12345 COMPUTERLAND 42561

Example of letterhead before formatting

5. Press [Ctrl] + [S] to save what you've done so far.
6. Format the text so that the letterhead name:
   • is in a much larger font than the other text;
   • has a font style of your choice;
   • is left-justified.
7. Drag the right-hand border of the first column to make it a wider column. (This is sometimes necessary to create more space for the company or personal name.)
8. Format your address so that it:
   • is right-justified in its own cell;
   • is in a smaller, plain font such as Arial, 9 point.
9. Remove all the borders from the table.
10. Press [Ctrl] + [S] to save what you've done so far.
11. Use the Menu Bar (**Format, Borders and Shading**) to make future borders bolder (1½ pt) and to change the colour to blue.
12. Use the ▦ **Outside Border** toolbar button to create a border below the last row.
13. Insert a Footer to include an item of text centred at the bottom of the page (for example Director's name/s, or your favourite quote if it's a personal letterhead).

14. Press `Ctrl` + `S` to save what you've done so far.
15. Format the text in Footer to how you want it.
16. View your letterhead in Print Preview and make any adjustments that you think are necessary.
17. Press `Ctrl` + `S` to save what you've done.
18. Print your letterhead.

LETTERHEAD NAME

P O Box 12345
COMPUTERLAND
42561

Example of letterhead after formatting

You can, of course, play around with the formatting and cell structure to get whatever effect you desire. Here are two other layouts you could try. The grey gridlines in the examples are to show you where the cell boundaries are. The blue lines indicate printable border lines.

LETTERHEAD NAME

| P O Box 12345, COMPUTERLAND, 42561 | Tel: 0123 456 7890 |

LETTERHEAD NAME

P O Box 12345	Tel: 0123 456 7890
COMPUTERLAND	Fax: 0123 456 7891
42561	E-mail: jody@amazulu.net

Other useful formatting methods

CREATING TWO OR MORE COLUMNS OF CONTINUOUS TEXT

When creating newsletters, brochures and other special documents you'll often need to divide the page into two or more columns. If you use a table, your text will all stay in the cell you're typing in and will not 'flow' into another column. To make the text flow continuously on the page and move into the next column when it reaches the end of the page, you'll need to use Word's **Columns** feature.

1. On the Word Standard Toolbar click on the
    ▦ **Columns** button and then in the little window
    to select how many columns you want.

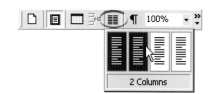

2. Start typing and when you reach the end of the first column your text will move up to the top of the second column.

Moving into the next column before the end of the page

On the Menu Bar click on **Insert**, then **Break**, then **Column Break**.
(Or press [Ctrl] + [Shift ⇧] + [Enter ↵].)

HAVING DIFFERENT LAYOUTS IN THE SAME DOCUMENT

If you want to have another part of the document (or page) with more or less columns, no columns, different page setups, and so on, you can do this by inserting a **Section break**. Each section can then be formatted as you wish.

1. On the Menu Bar click on **Insert**, then **Break**.
2. Click on the type of **Section break** you require. (**Continuous** will create a new section on the same page, where your cursor is flashing.)

ADDING USEFUL TOOLBARS WHEN NEEDED

Toolbars offer a quick and easy way of doing things, especially formatting text, creating a form, adding a text box, arrows, special shapes, and so on. Word has a good library of extra toolbars that can be used when needed.

Adding a specific toolbar

1. Start a new blank document.
2. **Right-click** on any blank place on the **Toolbar** at the top of Word, and a list of available toolbars will pop up.

Toolbars Menu

3. Click on **Drawing**, and the **Drawing Toolbar** will position itself at the top or bottom edge of the Word window, allowing you to add circles and ovals, rectangles and squares, various shapes of arrows, and so on.
4. On the **Drawing Toolbar** click on the little ⯆ drop-down arrow next to **AutoShapes** and a menu of AutoShapes will pop up showing ▶ sub-menu arrows.

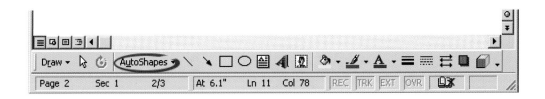

5. Point to each sub-menu to see what's available.

6. Click on a shape of your choice and it will attach itself invisibly to the mouse pointer, which will change into a + cross.

7. Click anywhere in your document and the AutoShape will position itself where you clicked on the page.

8. Press ⬚Del on a selected AutoShape to remove it from your document.

9. **Right-click** again on a blank area of the toolbar at the top of Word to call up the menu of available toolbars.

10. Click on **Drawing** again to deselect it, and the Drawing Toolbar will be removed from the Word window.

Decorating an AutoShape from the Drawing toolbar

You can decorate your AutoShapes with different colours and textures.

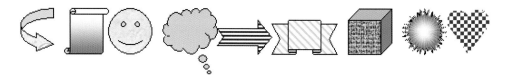

1. Follow the procedure explained above to show the **Drawing** toolbar and insert an AutoShape.

2. Click on the AutoShape to select it.

3. Then click the drop-down arrow next to the 🎨 ▾ **Fill Color** button to bring up the **Fill Color** menu.

4. To choose other colours or effects, click on **More Fill Colors** or **Fill Effects**.

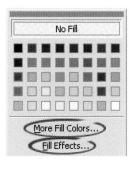

TIP:

You can change the size or proportions of an AutoShape by dragging one of its handles (the little white squares visible when the AutoShape is selected). You can also manage its size and shape before pasting it into the document. After selecting the shape, instead of clicking in the document to insert it in its default size, click and hold down the mouse button so that you can drag it to the required size while you are in the process of inserting it.

USING A TEXT BOX TO INSERT TEXT IN A SPECIFIC POSITION

You can position text or a picture anywhere on a page without being limited to the normal page layout of line spacing and so on. Word's **Text Box** is the solution. A text box can also lock an item in one position even when you type text above it in the body of the letter. This can be very useful when you wish to fix notes, pictures or other items permanently in a particular position on the page. Alternatively, you can wrap the text around the text box, which is useful for newsletters and the like, and the text box will move with the text if you type anything above it.

1. **Right-click** on a blank area in the Word Toolbar to open the list of available toolbars.
2. Click on **Drawing** and the Drawing Toolbar will position itself at the top or bottom edge of the Word window.

3. Click on the ▤ **Text Box** button and a text box will attach itself invisibly to the mouse pointer, which will change into a + cross.
4. Click anywhere in your document and the text box will position itself where you clicked on the page, in its default size and with the cursor already in the text box ready for you to type in it.
5. Type this in the text box: A text box is very useful for inserting text or a picture in a specific place in a document.

Changing the font properties (size, colour, style, and so on)
The text box will probably be too small for the text you have typed. So you'll need to resize either the text box or the font, depending on your needs. To change the size of the font:

1. Select the text by **triple-clicking** on it (clicking quickly on the text three times), or select the text using your favourite method.
2. Change the font properties in the usual way.

Resizing a text box to suit the contents

If the text box is too small or too large for what you want to include in it, you can simply resize it by dragging its borders or corners.

> Click on one of the text box's handles and hold down the mouse button so that you can drag the handle to change the box to the required size.

HINT:

This dragging procedure can also be done *while* you are in the process of inserting the text box. Once you've clicked on the **Text Box** button, instead of clicking once, click and drag to make it the required size. Try it now.

Formatting a text box

You can format a text box in many ways. For example, you can:

- show only the text, with no border visible;
- change the border to give it colour, make it bolder, and so on;
- give the Text Box a background shading;
- position the Text Box so that other text in the document wraps around it in the direction you specify.

Here's how to do it:

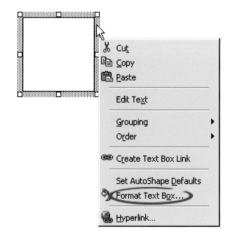

1. Click inside the text box to select it (there will be a grey border around it with white resizing handles).
2. **Right-click** anywhere on the grey border. The cursor will stop flashing and a menu will pop up.
3. Click on **Format Text Box** to open the **Format Text Box** dialog box.

4. Click on each tab and try out the various options available. Click on **OK** when you're done.

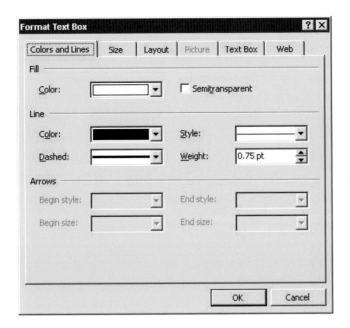

5. To remove a text box from a document, click on its **border**, then press [Del] . (Or right-click on the border, then click on **Cut**.)

ADDING PICTURES TO YOUR DOCUMENT

You can add saved photographs and other pictures to a Word document quite easily. If you don't have any of your own photographs saved to disk, then try out this procedure by using one of the samples usually provided by Windows.

Inserting a saved picture

1. Open a blank new Word document (or use an already open document) and click where you wish to place the picture.
2. On the Word Menu Bar click on **Insert** and point to **Picture**, and click on **From File** to open the **Insert Picture** dialog box.

3. Find the folder in which the picture is saved. If necessary, click on the ☝ **Up One Level** button to select the folder you need. (If you don't have your own picture, look for a folder named **Sample Pictures** and open it to select one of those supplied by Windows.)

4. Click on the file name in the left-hand pane to see a small preview of the picture in the right-hand pane.

5. When you have found the picture you want, click on **In̲sert** and the picture will be inserted into your document.

Resizing and aligning a picture

1. Click on the picture to select it, then click on its handles and drag it to the size you want.

2. To align the picture left, centred or right on the page, click on it to select it and then use the alignment shortcut of your choice, as you would do when aligning text (see page 73).

Formatting the picture layout

You can specify how you want the picture to relate to the text around it, and also choose other formatting options.

1. **Right-click** on the picture and a drop-down menu will pop up.
2. Click on **Format Picture** to open the **Format Picture** dialog box.
3. Click on the **Layout** tab and select the option of your choice.

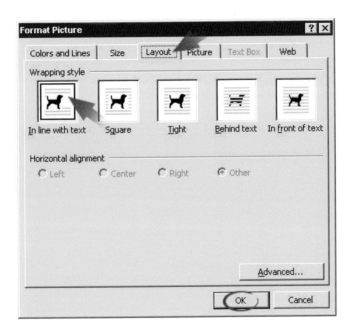

4. Click on each of the other tabs in turn to view the options and select the options of your choice.
5. Click on **OK** and the formatting you've selected will take effect.
6. If you want to delete the picture, click on it and press ![Del].

ADDING EXTRA BUTTONS TO THE WORD FORMATTING TOOLBAR

You can add additional formatting toolbar buttons to suit your personal needs. We'll demonstrate by adding a button for changing the case of a word or letter.

1. **Right-click** on a blank space on the Word Toolbar to call up the list of toolbars that are available.

2. Click on **Customize** and the **Customize** dialog box will open.

3. Click on the **Commands** tab.

4. In the left-hand **Categories:** pane, click on **Format**, and a list of formatting options will appear in the right-hand **Commands:** pane.

5. Click repeatedly on the bottom right-hand scroll arrow to view the items available, until you get to the item **Change Case**.

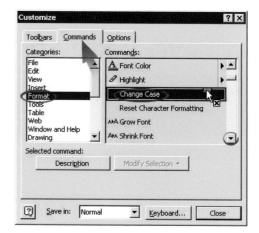

6. Click and hold down the mouse button to drag the item out of the dialog box and onto the Word Formatting Toolbar. Position it just after the three font formatting buttons. (When the pointer reaches the toolbar, a small vertical positioning line will appear as a guide to where the button will be positioned when you release the mouse button.)

7. When you're at the right place, release the mouse button and the new **Change Case** toolbar button will position itself on the Word Formatting Toolbar.

Deleting a button from the toolbar

1. Hold down the **Alt** key.
2. Click on the toolbar button you wish to remove and, holding down the mouse button, drag the toolbar button off the toolbar.

The button will disappear off the toolbar but will still be available on the **Commands** list in the **Customize** dialog box and can be added again later.

INSERTING SYMBOLS

Sometimes you might need to include in your document a special character that doesn't appear on your keyboard, for example the © or ™ characters, or even a little symbol such as a special arrow ⇨, or a pair of scissors ✄, or any one of a large library of symbols.

Inserting a symbol

1. On the Menu Bar click on **Insert**, then **Symbol**, and the **Symbol** dialog box will open at the **Symbols** tab.
2. In the **Font:** window click on the ▾ drop-down arrow to select the category of symbols you want to use. (**Monotype Sorts** and **Wingdings** offer some interesting symbols.)
3. Click on the symbol of your choice to see an enlarged view of it.
4. To insert it into the document, click on the **Insert** button or press **Enter**.
5. Click on **Enter** again or click on the **Close** button to return to the document.

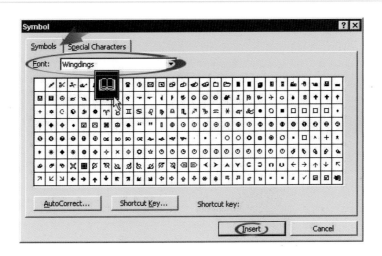

Inserting a special character (for example ©, ®, ™, ¶, —)

1. On the Menu Bar click on **<u>I</u>nsert**, then **<u>S</u>ymbol**, and the **Symbol** dialog box will open at the **<u>S</u>ymbols** tab.
2. Click on the **S<u>p</u>ecial Characters** tab.
3. Click repeatedly on the ⏷ bottom scrollbar arrow to browse through the items offered.
4. Click on the character of your choice and click on the **<u>I</u>nsert** button or press `Enter ↵` to insert it into the document.
5. Click on `Enter ↵` again or click on the **Close** button to return to the document.

If you apply all the knowledge you've gained about Microsoft Word from Books 1 and 2, you are well on your way to becoming an expert user of Word. To learn more about Word, remember to experiment and make good use of the `F1` **Help** facility to get the answers to your questions from Microsoft.

In the next chapter you'll learn useful tips about the Internet and e-mail management.

5 More on the Internet and e-mail

Here are some useful tips and tricks to get the most out of your time on the Internet – for both e-mail and for the World Wide Web. We'll start with the World Wide Web, which is a major part of 'The Internet' experience.

The Internet and World Wide Web

DELETING UNNECESSARY TEMPORARY FILES

Some Websites store small files in your computer system's temporary cache (memory) to speed up access to their Web pages. These automatically generated files accumulate over time and take up a vast amount of hard drive space if not deleted regularly, so it's a good idea to delete the temporary Internet files periodically.

1. In the Menu Bar click on **Tools**, then **Internet Options**, then on the **General** tab.

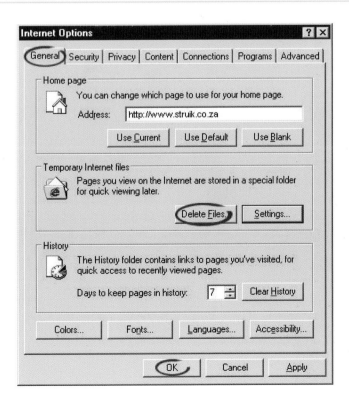

2. In the section under **Temporary Internet files**, click the **Delete File** button. A small window will open asking you for confirmation.

3. Click on the **Delete all offline content** option to enable it.
4. Click on **OK**, then click on **OK** in the dialog box to close it again.

PRINTING A WEB PAGE

Printing a Web page is much like printing any other document.

1. Press Ctrl + P to open the **Print** dialog box. Select the printing options and print the page.

If you have a version of Internet Explorer that offers a Print Preview option in the File menu, you can use this option before printing as explained below.

2. Click on **File**, then **Print Preview** to see what the printed page will look like.
3. If you want to change some settings such as margins, paper size, and so on, click on the 🔲 **Page Setup** button and make your choices, then click on **OK**.
4. Press Ctrl + P to open the **Print** dialog box. Select the printing options and print the page.

Saving ink by not printing background colours or images

Sometimes you may want to print only the text on the Web page and not the background colour or Web images. You can specify your requirements in Internet Explorer.

1. Click on **Tools**, then **Internet Options** to open the **Internet Options** dialog box.
2. Click on the **Advanced** tab and scroll down to the **Printing** item.
3. If the **Print background colors and images** item has a tick in it, click on it to remove the tick.
4. Click on **Apply**, then on **OK** and print the page as already explained.

NOTE:

Some Websites have a **Print this page** option (text or button) on the Web page itself.

To print, simply click on this text or button.

INSTANT MESSAGING WITH FRIENDS AROUND THE WORLD

Windows offers the opportunity to send and receive instant messages to and from friends or family around the world using what is called MSN Messenger, or Windows Messenger, depending on which version of Windows you have installed.

What this means is that when you are connected to the Internet you can type a message to another party who's online too and has the same program installed, and they can read it immediately and reply. So, in effect, you can have a conversation in text with one or more people all using the Messenger program. MSN Messenger has other features too. For example, you can:

- have a voice conversation over the Internet;
- have a video conversation;
- send files to each other;
- send a message to a mobile phone, and more.

MSN Messenger can open up a whole new world of global communication at the cost of a local telephone call while online. And the program itself is available free of charge. To get started, follow the procedure on the following page.

DOWNLOADING PROGRAMS FROM THE INTERNET

You can download many useful programs from Websites on the Internet and install them very easily onto your system. We'll explain using MSN Messenger as an example.

1. Open your browser and go to the 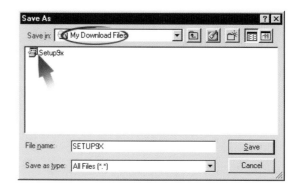 MSN Messenger Website at **http://messenger.msn.com**

2. Click the **Download Now** icon on the Website and in the dialog box that opens select the option to **save** the file to your computer. The **Save As** dialog box will open. (You may get a window that asks if you'd like to **Run this program from its current location** OR **Save this program to disk**. Select **Save this program to disk**. Then the **Save As** dialog box will open.)

TIP:

Downloaded files are often automatically directed to the **My Download Files** folder on the **[C:]** drive. However, if your **Save As** dialog box doesn't offer this folder it is a good idea to create it on your **[C:]** drive using the **Save As** procedures explained on page 43. This is better than saving it to your Desktop, which is an option sometimes offered.

3. Make a note of the file name so you will recognize it when you go later to the **My Download Files** folder to install the program.

4. Click on the **Save** button.

TIP:

To make things easier for yourself, make a practice of saving downloaded files to the **My Download Files** folder.

Installing a downloaded program

After clicking **Download Now** on the MSN Messenger Website, a new Web page will automatically open with step-by-step instructions on how to install MSN Messenger and how to set up your new Messenger. If this doesn't happen, you can install the program easily yourself as follows:

1. Use Windows Explorer to find the file (the one you made a note of on page 94).
2. **Double-click** on it to open it, and follow the prompts.

Finding other download sites

Here's a quick way to find more downloadable programs.

1. In your browser (for example Internet Explorer), go to the search engine Google Website at **http://www.google.com**
2. In the blank search window near the top, type in the word downloads.
3. Click on the **Google Search** button and a list of download sites will be displayed.

The three categories of downloadable offerings are:

1. FREEWARE	Programs that are offered free of charge, no strings attached.
2. SHAREWARE	Programs that are offered on a free trial basis, usually for 30 days, after which you are expected to make a payment for continued use of the program.
3. COMMERCIAL	Programs that can be purchased online from the supplier. These include 'evaluation' programs, where you can try out the program for 30 days before paying for it. Once the evaluation period has expired, the program usually won't continue functioning until you make a payment.

Some useful programs to download

Hundreds of programs are available for download on the Internet. Some of these can be pretty useful, while others can be regarded as essential, such as a **zip** program for opening compressed or 'zipped' files, and Acrobat Reader, which is needed for opening files in Portable Document Format (**PDF**).

1. While 'online', go to **http://www.google.com** and search for "Acrobat Reader".
2. Follow the links to the download page to obtain the free program from the Adobe Website.
3. Do a different search for "zip files" and follow the links to a download page for a suitable zip program such as **WinZip**.
4. Visit the Website of this book at **http://www.reallyeasycomputerbooks.com** and find the links to other useful downloadable programs and download Websites.

DOWNLOAD PRECAUTION

Be cautious when downloading from a Website. Learn to recognize which sites are considered safe.

REMOVING INSTALLED PROGRAMS

Sometimes you may no longer need a program that you've installed, and therefore need to remove it from your system. Or you might need to reinstall a program that has corrupted or is malfunctioning, in which case it must first be uninstalled. Here's how to uninstall a program.

1. Click on **Start**, then **Settings**, then **Control Panel**.
2. **Double-click** on the Add/Remove Programs icon to open the **Add/Remove Programs Properties** dialog box.
3. Click on the program you want to uninstall.
4. Click on the **Add/Remove** button and follow the prompts.

WHEN INSTALLING OR UNINSTALLING

When installing or uninstalling programs (software) or equipment (hardware), it is important to do the following:

1. **Beforehand:** Always save any data in open programs, then close all programs before installing or uninstalling.
2. **Afterwards:** Always restart your computer when the installing or uninstalling is complete.

E-mail with Outlook Express

E-mail was extensively covered in Book 1, but here are some additional useful things to help make your e-mailing life simpler with the popular e-mail program, **Outlook Express**.

SETTING RULES FOR AUTOMATIC MAIL HANDLING

With **Message Rules**, you can tell Outlook Express how to handle mail to or from a particular sender, or where the subject line contains certain text, and so on. Based on the rules you set, such mail can be sent immediately to a specified folder, or deleted, forwarded, deleted from the mail server without being downloaded to your computer, and so on. This can be very useful in helping to reduce the amount of organizing you need to do manually, especially if you have quite a lot of e-mail movement each day.

1. On the Menu Bar click on **Tools**, point to **Rules** and click on **Mail**, to open the **New Mail Rule** dialog box.

NOTE:

If rules have already been set up, then to add a new one after clicking on **Mail** in Step 1 above, you will need to click on **New** in order to open the **New Mail Rule** dialog box.

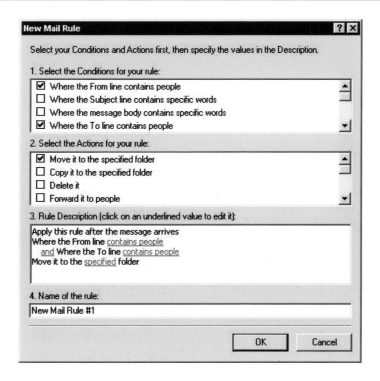

2. Scroll through the list of **Conditions** in pane number 1, and select at least one, but more if you wish.

3. Do the same for the **Actions** in pane number 2. (As each item is checked, a hyperlink will appear in the last pane.)

4. Next, click on each underlined hyperlink in pane number 3 to enter the specific conditions or actions for your rule. (This will be for this particular rule only. You can add more new rules using this same procedure.)

5. Lastly, in pane number 4 enter a brief description of this rule, or simply accept what's offered by Outlook Express.

6. Click on **OK** and your rule will apply to future incoming or outgoing e-mails affected by this rule.

USING SIGNATURES IN OUTGOING MAIL

A **signature** is simply a pretyped piece of text that can be added automatically at the end of your outgoing e-mail letters. You can create several signatures: for your personal use, business, club and so on. You can also format the signatures as you wish.

1. On the Outlook Express main Menu Bar, click on **Tools**, then on **Options**.

2. In the **Options** dialog box that opens, click on the **Signatures** tab.

3. Click on the **New** button.

4. In the **Edit Signature** pane type the signature you require.

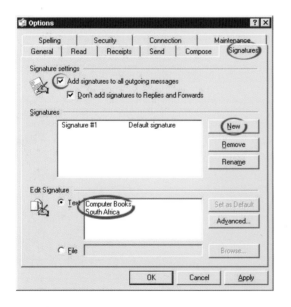

5. To have the signature appear on all outgoing e-mails, click the check box next to **Add signatures to all outgoing messages.**

6. Click on **Apply**, then on **OK**.

SENDING ONE MAIL PRIVATELY TO SEVERAL PEOPLE

People have a right to the privacy of their e-mail addresses. So when sending the same letter to a number of people in one e-mail transmission, it is good practice to protect the privacy of every recipient by not allowing them to see the list of e-mail addresses to whom you sent the e-mail.

Creating a special Address Book entry

1. Create an entry in your Address Book with a name that you can easily recognise, for example Book Club (or any other name you like).
2. Use your own e-mail address for this entry, click on **Add**, then on **OK**.

PREPARATION FOR THE NEXT STEP:

Make sure that your new message shows the 📧 Bcc: button above the **Subject:** line.

If not, in the Menu Bar click on **View**, then on **All Headers**.

Addressing the e-mail

1. When preparing your new message, click on 📧 To: and, in the **Select Recipients** dialog box that opens, select your special address book entry and click on To: -> to send the recipient to the top right-hand pane. The dialog box will stay open.

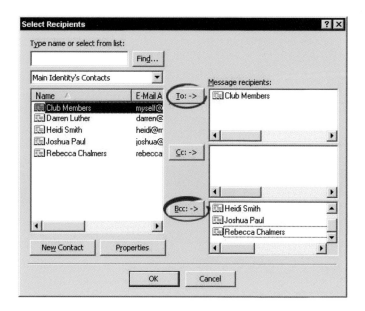

2. Next, hold down the `Ctrl` key and click on each recipient who will receive your e-mail, then release the `Ctrl` key.
3. Click on the `Bcc: ->` button to send these names to the Bcc pane on the right. (Bcc means blind carbon copy – recipients will not be able to see who received the e-mail.)
4. Then click on **OK** to return to your e-mail message and type your letter.

EXPLORING OTHER ASPECTS OF PERSONALIZING YOUR E-MAILS

1. While in Outlook Express, press `F1`, then click on the **Index** tab.
2. Type in the keyword `signatures`.
3. In the list that appears, **double-click** on **signatures, personal** and read the information in the right-hand pane.
4. Click on the **Related Topics** hyperlink for additional things you can do.
5. Repeat the process by looking up other keywords that interest you.

PROTECTING YOUR COMPUTER AGAINST THE DREADED VIRUS PROBLEM

A 'virus' is a program maliciously designed to do damage to computer systems. It can duplicate itself from file to file and from computer to computer, and can therefore cause havoc by quickly spreading through many systems and networks to 'infect' a large number of computer systems worldwide. These are nasty little things that you need to take precautions to avoid. They can be spread via infected CDs, floppy disks or infected e-mails, and by downloading something from a risky Website or even directly through your Internet connection without your knowledge.

These days, no-one should be without an effective anti-virus program that is kept updated frequently (i.e. weekly or even daily) to deal with these nasties as soon as they are detected.

Popular brands of anti-virus programs include Norton, McAfee and Trend Micro PC-cillin who go one step further and offer a free online virus scan service.

To get more information on virus protection:

1. Speak to a reliable computer technician, OR
2. Use **www.google.com** and in the search window type "anti-virus" and press `Enter` or click on the **Google Search** button. Visit some of the links found.

Immediate precautions to take

- Install a reliable anti-virus program as a matter of urgency.
- Make sure your anti-virus program offers an online service that updates your 'virus definitions' whenever you are connected to the Internet. This will ensure that you are always protected against the latest known viruses.
- Before using any data on a computer CD or floppy disk obtained from someone else, use your anti-virus program to do a virus scan on it to make sure that it is free of any viruses.
- Renew your subscription (usually annually) to stay up-to-date with anti-virus program updates and virus definition updates.
- Don't open attachments in e-mails from people you don't know – in fact, no attachments should be opened if you don't have an anti-virus program. Many viruses forge e-mail addresses, so what you 'might' think is an e-mail coming from a friend, may be a virus-laden e-mail.

 PERSONAL INTERNET SECURITY
Being connected to the Internet means you are connected to millions of computers all around the world, and millions of other Internet users. This makes you vulnerable to invasion of your privacy and security, and it is wise not to be too trusting. Here are some tips to help you protect your privacy and general safety:

- **Don't take chances with viruses. Protect your system now!**
- **Don't give your personal details (for example telephone numbers, physical address, banking details) to strangers in chat rooms, instant messaging systems, in response to unsolicited e-mails, and so on.**
- **Don't give out credit card details unless you know the Website is secure.**
- **If you get junk mail (called spam mail in Internet jargon) just trash it. Don't fall for the enticing invitations, and don't respond in anger by telling them not to send you their junk. And don't click on any 'Unsubscribe' links. Doing this simply confirms to the sending system that your e-mail address is active and you'll stay on their mailing list.**
- **Sign up for a free Web-based e-mail address with Yahoo or Hotmail, so that you have an alternative e-mail address. Then, when you need to give an e-mail address for special offers, Internet subscription services and so on, you can use your alternative Web-based address so that your regular e-mail address with your service provider does not become a target for spam mail.**
- **Visit our Website at www.reallyeasycomputerbooks.com for useful links to free anti-spam programs that you can download and install.**

6 Keeping your system efficient

> **!** This chapter is extremely important, so do read it carefully and follow the procedures given.

GOOD HOUSEKEEPING PRACTICES

Keep the area around your computer clean and dust-free as computers have fans that draw air inside the case to cool the internal components. If the environment where your computer is set up is dusty, vacuum the vents on the front, side and rear of the computer on a regular basis.

Avoid eating or drinking near your computer. Spilled drinks are the number one cause of malfunctioning keyboards. Food crumbs may get into the mouse and cause excessive wear and tear of the rollers, necessitating cleaning or replacement of the mouse.

REGULAR SERVICING PROCEDURES

Every now and then you should clean up your hard drive by doing some minor disk maintenance. Some say weekly, others say monthly. It depends on how much you use your computer. The three basic procedures given below should keep your computer clean and happy for a while. This will also speed things up, because clutter and fragmentation do slow down a PC's performance. So, follow these three maintenance procedures regularly.

Deleting unneeded files from the hard disk
Windows stores temporary files on your system which, over time, can accumulate and take up much needed disk space. It's a good idea to delete these frequently to free up disk space and speed up your system.

1. Click on , then **Programs**, then **Accessories**, then **System Tools**, then **Disk Cleanup**.
2. Select **Drive [C:]**.
3. Tick the following items to be cleaned: **Temporary Internet Files**, **Recycle Bin**, and **Temporary Files**.

4. **Don't** tick **Downloaded Program Files** in case you need to reinstall one of them again later.
5. Click on **OK** and, in the confirmation box that pops up, click on **Yes**.

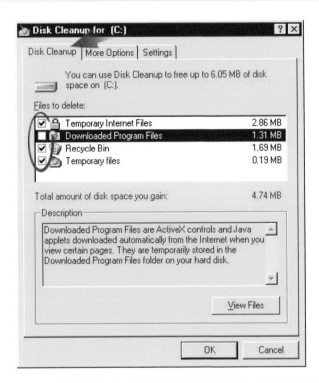

TIP:

When you're finished cleaning up your drive, it's good practice to run ScanDisk.

Running ScanDisk to check for errors on the hard disk

1. Close all applications (programs) before starting **ScanDisk**.
2. Click on [🏁Start] , then **Programs**, **Accessories**, **System Tools**, and **ScanDisk**.
3. Select **[C:]** if it's not already highlighted.
4. Choose **Standard** setting, unless you suspect actual physical damage to your hard drive surface. Then, and only then, use the **Thorough** option and ScanDisk will check for this possibility.
5. If ScanDisk's **Thorough** option does find physical damage, back up your information as soon as possible and take your computer into a service centre to have it checked.

6. Click **Automatically fix errors**.

7. Click on **<u>S</u>tart** and leave your computer alone while it does this task. This may take a few minutes (or up to several hours if you choose the **<u>T</u>horough** option).

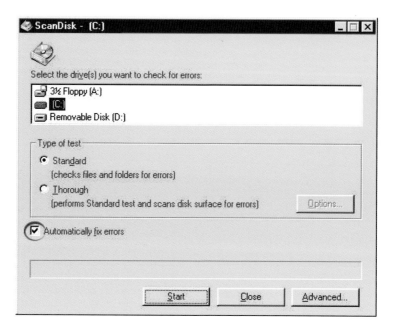

 ScanDisk will display a report at the end of the scanning and fixing process. If it reports any **bad sectors**, beware! This means that your hard disk (drive) is damaged and could 'crash' at any time and take all your data with it. Create a backup of your key data files and immediately arrange for your computer to be checked by a competent technician.

Running Disk Defragmenter to speed up file access

Defragmentation is another tool you should use regularly, although it's more for performance improvement than problem solving like ScanDisk. 'Defrag' rearranges file storage as files and empty spaces become scattered across the drive over time. To keep your drive running efficiently run **Disk Defragmenter** frequently, depending on your computer usage – at least monthly – and also each time after running ScanDisk.

1. First do a ScanDisk to fix any disk errors on your hard drive.

2. With all programs still closed, **right-click** on each item on the right-hand side of the Taskbar to disable any items that might try to write to the hard drive during the defragging process (for example Task Scheduler, any Anti-Virus button).

3. Click on , then **P**rograms, then **Accessories**, then **System Tools**, then **Disk Defragmenter**. When the **Select Drive** dialog box pops up, make sure it's set to defrag **Drive C Physical drive**.

4. Click on **OK** and a small **Defragmenting Drive C** window will open showing you the progress of the defrag.

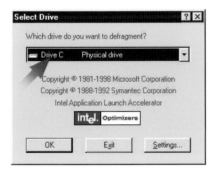

5. Leave the computer to do its thing until it's finished. If you continue to work on your computer during defragmentation, every time you input more data to the hard drive, defrag will start over, so walk away from the computer and leave it be. This might take quite a while (30–90 minutes or more, depending on how much fragmentation you have on your hard drive and on how big your hard drive is). It will tell you when it's done.

6. Reboot (restart) your computer after defragging.

If you're curious to see the details of the process, click on the **Show Details** button in the **Defragmenting Drive C** dialog box. Be aware though, that by showing details, the Defrag process will take much longer. But if you have nothing better to do on a Friday night, by all means click on **Show Details** and you'll find yourself sitting in front of your computer, mesmerized by the defragging process ☺.

NOTE:
You can also do an all-in-one maintenance by following the procedure on page 106.

1. Click on ![Start], then **Programs**, then **Accessories**, then **System Tools**, then **Maintenance Wizard**.

2. Make sure the radio button **Perform maintenance now** is highlighted. If not, click on it.

3. Click on **OK**.

4. Leave your computer to go through the maintenance routine, which could take over an hour. Check every now and then to see if there are any error messages, and follow any prompts.

IF YOUR COMPUTER MALFUNCTIONS

Sometimes a warning message will appear on your screen telling you that the program has performed an illegal operation. Or you may find that everything 'freezes' on your screen and nothing seems to be responding, sometimes not even the mouse. Don't panic. Do the following if you get these messages:

If the program you're using malfunctions
Sometimes you'll get an error message saying that the program you're using has performed an **Illegal Operation**.

1. Follow any prompts in the warning message that pops up.

2. Wait a while (about a minute or two), and see if things correct themselves.

3. If a **Close Program** dialog box pops up, see if it states that the program is not responding.

4. If so, click on the **End Task** button.

5. If there is no dialog box, press [Ctrl] + [Alt] + [Del] all at the same time and hold each key down. A **Close Program** dialog box should pop up.
6. Now release the three keys.

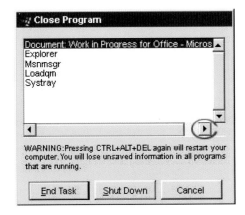

7. On the bottom scroll bar of the dialog box, click on the arrow on the right so that you can read the whole line above for the program you've been working in.
8. If it states that the program is **not responding**, click on the **<u>E</u>nd Task** button and wait while the program shuts down.
9. Reload the program and continue working in it.

 If you have something very important that has not been saved, you may want to wait a while longer to see if the system responds later by itself. That way you won't lose any unsaved changes. If nothing happens after a while, give up and click on **<u>E</u>nd Task**.

If the program won't shut down

1. Click on the **<u>S</u>hut Down** button next to the **<u>E</u>nd Task** button. Your computer should then restart (reboot), and you will lose any unsaved changes.
2. Wait while the computer restarts. It may automatically go through the **ScanDisk** routine to fix any errors on the system.

If the computer won't restart

1. Press `Ctrl` + `Alt` + `Del` twice in succession to restart the computer.
2. If that also doesn't work, click on the **Reset** button on the computer box or tower. (This is often a small recessed button that needs to be pressed in with an object such as a ballpoint pen. Modern computers often have a reset button that can be pressed with a finger.)
3. Wait while the computer restarts. It may automatically go through the **ScanDisk** routine to fix any errors in the system.

Everything 'freezes', even the mouse won't respond

1. Follow the same procedures as above, in sequence, to restart the computer.
2. Try the `Ctrl` + `Alt` + `Del` procedure several times, and your system might shut down and restart.
3. If absolutely nothing at all helps, not even the **Reset** button, then you have only one choice left: press the **POWER OFF** switch on your computer to switch it off.
4. Wait a minute or so to allow the hard disk to stop spinning, then turn the power switch back on and wait while your computer boots up and possibly performs a **ScanDisk** routine to fix any errors.
5. Follow any instructions on the screen.

A program starts doing strange things

1. Save your changes and exit the program, then re-open it.
2. If it still behaves strangely, or if other programs also seem to be acting unusually, then it's best to save your data and exit all programs, then restart the computer.
3. Click on `Start` , **Sh<u>u</u>t Down**, **<u>R</u>estart**, and wait for the computer to reboot.

The computer seems to become very slow

Sometimes Windows 98 will give a message that there is insufficient memory available to complete a task. This means that many of the system's available resources have been gobbled up by programs that have been running. Symptoms can include: slow performance, error messages or programs not responding properly. To fix this problem, restart Windows.

7 Introducing spreadsheets (Excel)

The popular Microsoft spreadsheet program is called Excel. Excel allows you to do a great many calculations with columns and numbers that would normally be very time-consuming if done with a calculator and a paper spreadsheet. This can be a great advantage for such number-based information as:

- home or business budgets;
- basic accounting;
- sales and profit data and graphic charts;
- statistical analysis, and so on.

In addition, you can use Excel to generate fancy and professional bar charts, graphs and other graphic representations of your data.

This is all done in what are called Worksheets, the advantage of which is that if you want to change one number – a percentage, a value, or a time-period, and so on – the formulas in the worksheet will automatically recalculate all the other data for you.

So, let's take a look at how Excel works.

STARTING A NEW WORKSHEET IN A NEW WORKBOOK

1. Click on **Start**, then **Programs**, then on **Microsoft Excel** to open Excel.

NOTE:
If you think you'll be using Excel frequently, remember to right-click on Microsoft Excel in the Programs menu, then click on **Send To**, then **Desktop (create shortcut)** to place a shortcut on your Desktop, which can be dragged onto the Quick Launch Toolbar.

Excel will open and display a new Worksheet ready for your data input. Notice that the toolbars are in many ways similar to those of Word. The Worksheet is made up columns and rows, which in turn make up the many cells available for inserting information or data. The cell in the top left-hand corner has bold borders to indicate that it is selected and ready for having data typed into it.

Before you start, let's give the Workbook a name, instead of its present temporary name, Book1.

2. Press $\boxed{\text{Ctrl}}$ + $\boxed{\text{S}}$, as you've done before to save a Word document, and the **Save As** dialog box will open.

3. Browse to find the folder **Computer Exercises** and select it, as already explained in Chapter 3, so that it appears in the **Save in:** window.

4. In the **File name:** text window type MyFirstWorkbook.

5. Click on **Save** or press $\boxed{\text{Enter}}$. The new file name will now appear in the Title Bar.

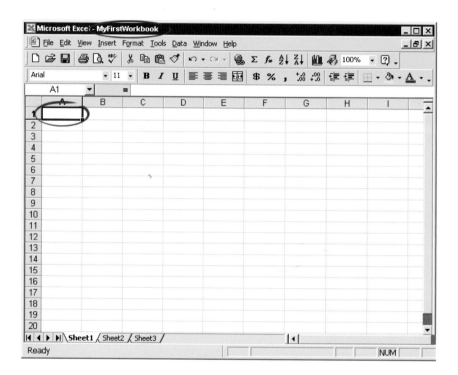

Naming a Worksheet

1. Right-click on the tab at the bottom left that says **Sheet1**.

2. In the menu that pops up, click on **Rename** and **Sheet1** will be selected for overtyping.

3. Type the words Home Budget and press $\boxed{\text{Enter}}$. The sheet will now have that name.

Note that there are additional sheets available too, and you can add even more sheets to the Workbook via **Insert**, **Worksheet** on the Menu Bar.

MOVING THROUGH COLUMNS AND ROWS

Where you want to go:	What to do to get there:
➤ To next cell on the right	`Tab` key or the `→` right arrow key
◄ To next cell to the left	`←` left arrow key
▼ To next cell down	`Enter` or `↓` down arrow key
▲ To next cell up	`↑` up arrow key
✥ To any cell	Click in the cell
⊢◄ To first column, same row	`Hom` key

ENTERING DATA INTO CELLS

1. If not preselected, click to select the first cell (Column A, Row 1) and type the words: My Home Budget, then press `Enter`. (Notice how the text extends beyond the border of the cell and that the cell name is also displayed in the Name Box above cell A1.)
2. Click in that first cell (A1) again to select it.
3. On the Formatting Toolbar click on the **Font Size** ▾ arrow and click on **14** to make the heading bigger.
4. Click on the **B** button to make the title **bold**.
5. Click on the ▾ drop-down arrow next to the **A ▾** **Font Color** toolbar button and click on the red box to make the heading red.
6. Press `Enter` to give effect to the formatting changes. (The cell selection will jump to the next cell down, cell A2.)

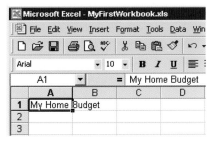

Before formatting

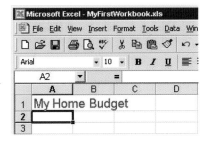

After formatting

7. Now type the following headings in the cells shown in the illustration below.

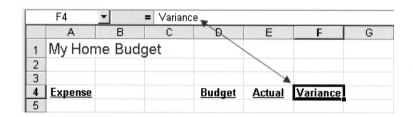

8. Use your knowledge of Word to centre and format the headings as shown.

TIP:

The contents of a cell are displayed in the long window above the column names (called the Formula Bar). You can edit the contents by clicking and typing your corrections in that window.

9. Next, select each cell in turn and type in the text and numbers as shown below.

	A	B	C	D	E	F	G
1	My Home Budget						
2							
3							
4	**Expense**			**Budget**	**Actual**	**Variance**	
5							
6	Rent			1000	1001		
7	Car			1000	950		
8	School Fees			200	220		
9	Housekeeping			1200	1300		
10	Total						
11							

Now we need to tell Excel what those numbers represent, such as straightforward Numbers, Currencies, Dates, Percentages, and so on. We first need to select the cells involved so that we can specify the number type for those cells.

SELECTING A RANGE OF CELLS

1. Click in cell **D6** (column **D**, row **6**) and hold down the mouse button.
2. Now drag the pointer to the right to select **columns D to F**, and down to select **rows 6 to 10**.
3. Release the mouse button and that block of cells will now be selected.

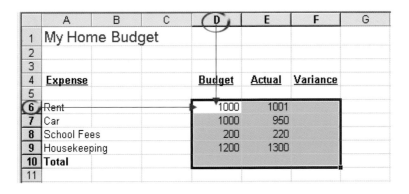

SPECIFYING DATA FORMATS

1. In the Menu Bar, click on **Format**, then on **Cells** and the **Format Cells** dialog box will open.

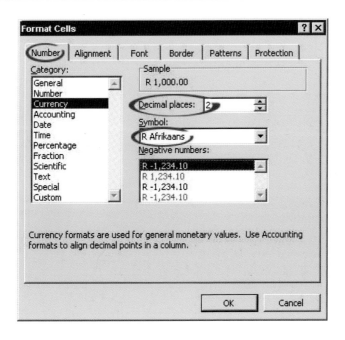

2. For these cells click on **Currency**, set the **Decimal places:** to **2**, and choose the currency of your country.

3. Click on **OK**. (You won't see the effect of the formatting in columns **F** and **G** because there isn't any data in those cells yet.)

NOTE:

If you see a whole lot of these ######### in a cell, it means the column is too narrow to display all the data in it. To fix this, click on the right border in the top grey bar of that column, and with the mouse button held down, drag the column border a little to the right until all the contents are visible.

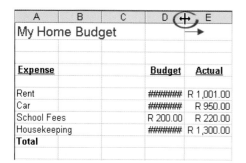

Before expanding column width

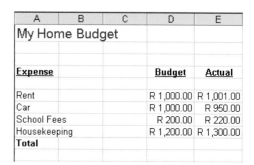

After expanding column width

GETTING EXCEL TO DO YOUR CALCULATIONS FOR YOU

Here comes the fun part. We're going to get Excel to do some calculations for us.

1. Click in cell **D10** to select it.
2. In the **Standard Toolbar** click on the Σ **AutoSum** button and the formula for automatic additions will appear in the cell and also in the Formula Bar (long window) above.

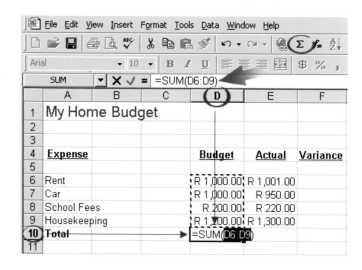

---

3. Press [Enter⏎] and the selected cell will display the sum of the adjacent numbers above it.

4. Next, to duplicate the formula for cell **E10**, click on the **Fill Handle** on the bottom right corner of cell **D10** (see right) and, holding the mouse button down, drag the handle to cell **E10**.

Budget	Actual
R 1,000.00	R 1,001.00
R 1,000.00	R 950.00
R 200.00	R 220.00
R 1,200.00	R 1,300.00
R 3,400.00	

5. Release the mouse button and the formula will be pasted into **E10** to give the sum of the numbers above it.

Budget	Actual
R 1,000.00	R 1,001.00
R 1,000.00	R 950.00
R 200.00	R 220.00
R 1,200.00	R 1,300.00
R 3,400.00	R 3,471.00

Now let's see how much the actual expenditure varies from the budget. To do this we need to calculate the difference between column D and column E, line by line, and in total.

6. Click in cell **F6** to select it.

7. Click on the [=] **equals sign** on the left of the Formula Bar and an = **equals sign** will appear in the cell and also in the Formula Bar.

8. Click in cell **D6**, and notice that the cell reference appears in cell **F6** and in the Formula Bar where the cursor is flashing.

9. Now, type a – **minus sign** in the Formula Bar.

10. Now click in cell **E6** to tell Excel that this is the number that must be subtracted from the number in **D6**.

11. Press [Enter⏎] and the formula will calculate the answer and display in it cell **F6**.

Budget	Actual	Variance
R 1,000.00	R 1,001.00	-R 1.00
R 1,000.00	R 950.00	
R 200.00	R 220.00	
R 1,200.00	R 1,300.00	
R 3,400.00	R 3,471.00	

COPYING A FORMULA TO OTHER CELLS

Now we need to duplicate the formula for the remaining rows of numbers in that column so that we can get the answers for each line and also the total.

1. Click in cell **F6** to select it.
2. Click on the Fill Handle and drag it downwards to cell **F10**. The formula will now be duplicated for each row and the answers displayed in each cell.
3. Click anywhere outside the selected area to de-select it.

Budget	Actual	Variance
R 1,000.00	R 1,001.00	-R 1.00
R 1,000.00	R 950.00	R 50.00
R 200.00	R 220.00	-R 20.00
R 1,200.00	R 1,300.00	-R 100.00
R 3,400.00	R 3,471.00	-R 71.00

NOTE:
When you duplicate a formula in this way, Excel automatically adjusts the formula to make it applicable for each row (or column, as the case may be).

You now have a table showing by item, the budget, the actual, and the variance between the two. Now, let's depict this in a fancy chart.

CREATING CHARTS OF YOUR DATA

Excel will create a professional chart for you from the data you select, and offers a variety of chart styles from which to choose.

1. Click in cell **A4** and hold down the mouse button while you drag the pointer to the right and downwards until all the cells from **A4 to F10** are selected.
2. Release the mouse button.

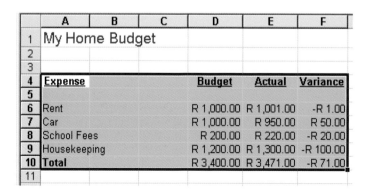

	A	B	C	D	E	F
1	My Home Budget					
2						
3						
4	Expense			Budget	Actual	Variance
5						
6	Rent			R 1,000.00	R 1,001.00	-R 1.00
7	Car			R 1,000.00	R 950.00	R 50.00
8	School Fees			R 200.00	R 220.00	-R 20.00
9	Housekeeping			R 1,200.00	R 1,300.00	-R 100.00
10	Total			R 3,400.00	R 3,471.00	-R 71.00
11						

3. In the Standard Toolbar click on the  **Chart Wizard** button to open the **Chart Wizard** dialog box at Step 1 of 4.

You can scroll through the various styles in the **Chart type:** pane on the left to select any suitable style of your choice. For this example we'll accept the chart style offered by Excel.

4. Click on the **Next >** button to move to Step 2 of 4.

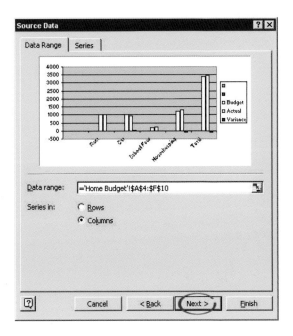

5. Accept what's offered in the Step 2 dialog box and click on **Next >** to move to Step 3.
6. In the **Chart title:** window of the Step 3 dialog box type the name you want to give your chart: Home Budget.
7. In the **Category (X) axis:** window type the word Item.
8. In the **Value (Y) axis:** window type the word Rand (or whichever currency you use in your country).

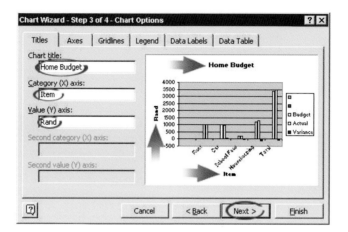

9. Click on **Next >** to move to Step 4 of 4.
10. Click in the radio button next to **As new sheet:** so that the chart will be a separate sheet and not added as a graphic chart into the main worksheet.
11. Type Home Budget Chart in the **As new sheet:** window.

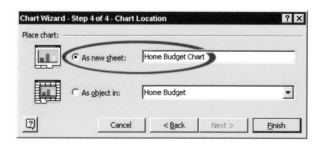

12. Click on the **Finish** button and the new chart will be displayed as a full page, with its tab selected in the Excel status bar at the bottom.

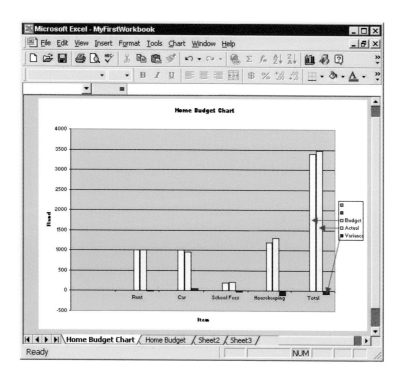

You can choose from a variety of chart types available in the Step 1 of 4 dialog box. Here are two further examples.

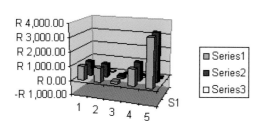

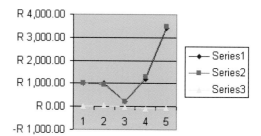

Excel offers a wide range of features for working with numbers. These include:
• formatting cells, columns, rows, text, and the general appearance of a Worksheet;
• linking Worksheets so that if a number on one sheet is changed, Excel will recalculate all the numbers in the linked sheet as well, based on the changes in the first sheet, or in any linked formula;
• doing highly sophisticated calculations and comparisons, and much more.

SOME USEFUL THINGS TO KNOW ABOUT EXCEL

Working in cells

In order to:	Do this:
Work in a cell	Click in the cell to select it
Delete a cell's contents	Select the cell and press Del
Copy data from cell to cell	Select the cell and use the copy-and-paste method (see page 48)
Select a range of cells	Select the first cell and drag the pointer over the other cells you want to select
Format the contents or appearance of a cell	Select the cell/s and: Use the buttons in the Formatting Toolbar OR Click on the **Format** menu and make your choices
To move a cell's contents to another cell	1. Click in the cell to select it. 2. Click on the left-hand top corner of the cell and drag it to the destination cell. 3. Release the mouse button.

TAKING EXCEL FURTHER:

Use Excel's F1 Help feature to find out more, and experiment with the various items on the Menu Bar and the different toolbar buttons. Also refer to the table on the next page. Have fun!

Using formulas

In order to:	Use this:	And do this:
Enter a formula	=	Select the cell and type an equals sign (or click on the ◻= **Edit Formula** button to the left of the Formula Bar), then type the formula into the Formula Bar, OR use the Σ **AutoSum** button.
Copy a cell's formula or format		1. Select and click on the ▤ **Copy** button on the Standard Toolbar to copy the source cell's data. 2. Click on **Edit**, **Paste Special** and make your selection/s. (Excel will adjust the copied formula to change to the applicable row.)
Keep an element of a formula constant	$	In the Formula Bar type a $ sign before the cell column and/or row reference, for example **E4*D9** (Column E and Row 4 will remain constant even if you copy the formula to another cell).
Add the data in two or more cells	+	Type a + sign between the cell references in the Formula Bar, then press ⌨Enter , for example **=A4+B7**
Multiply the data in two or more cells	*	Type an asterisk (*) between the cell references in the Formula Bar, for example **=A1*E16**
Subtract data	–	Type a minus (-) sign between the cell references, as applicable, for example **=A1-E16**
Divide one cell's data by another's	/	Type a forward slash (/) before the denominator, for example **=A4/B7**
Express a percentage	%	After creating your formula, select the cell/s and click on the % button. Use ◻F1 for more on the decimal points in percentages.
Automatically add	Σ	Click on Σ **AutoSum**, then on the ▾ next to the word **SUM** on the left of the **Formula Toolbar** and select the option you require.
Create more complicated formulas	( )	Place each component within brackets, for example **=(B6+C6+D6)*(F14+G14+H14)**
Specify a range of cells in a formula	:	Type a colon between the first and last cell, for example the formula in the item above could read as **=(B6:D6)*(F14:H14)**

8 Introducing some other programs

This chapter will give you a brief overview of some of the other programs that come bundled with Microsoft Office and with the Windows operating system. More detailed knowledge can be obtained via the Help menus of each program, and also from program-specific books.

So, let's take a look at some of these other programs.

Slide presentations with PowerPoint

Gone are the days when you needed to get a professional advertising agency to make your slide shows for you from 35 mm slide photos. With PowerPoint you can do it all on your own computer – very easily. You can create professional, full-colour slide presentations that can be projected onto a projection screen or viewed by others on their own computers via a CD.

In **Sli̱de Sorter View**, you can sort your slides, copy and paste new slides, and import slides from other presentations.

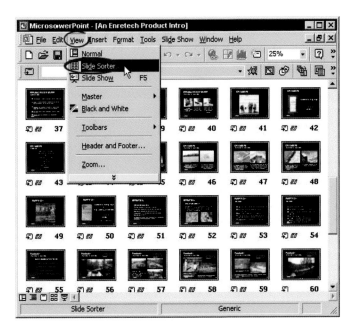

In **Slide Sho̱w View**, you can view a full-screen slide show on your computer screen, or have it projected onto a projection screen.

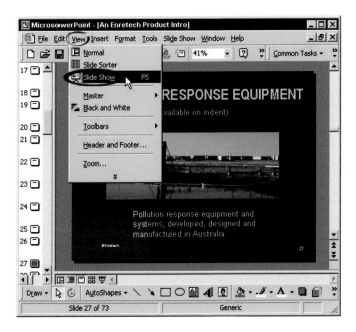

PowerPoint also offers views for creating and editing the slides, and for organising presentation content in an organized outline of heading and text structure, and so on.

You can also **animate** your slide show with visual movement, introducing lines and bullet points one by one with motion, and moving from one slide to another. And you can add sound effects too.

CREATING A NEW PRESENTATION

1. Click on ⊞Start, then **Programs**, then on ▣ **Microsoft PowerPoint** to open PowerPoint. The **PowerPoint** dialog box will open.
2. Click on **AutoContent Wizard**, then click on **OK** to start the wizard.
3. Follow the prompts and experiment with the various options offered.

4. When done, close the document and start a new one by clicking on the ▯ **New** button on the Standard Toolbar to open the **New Slide** dialog box, and experiment via that method.

Additional guidance can be obtained from the ▣ Help facility in PowerPoint.

Working with databases in Access

If you ever have a need to work with data records, Microsoft's program called Access is the one to use. It comes as part of the Microsoft Office suite and is used for such record management as:
- name and address lists;
- employee, customer or club member details;
- forms to show each person's stored data;
- reports showing the data according to criteria specified by you;
- printing mailing labels.

1. Click on **Start**, then **Programs**, then on **Microsoft Access** to open Access.
2. Click on **File**, then **New** to start a new database, and try out the various tabs and options offered in the **New** dialog box.
3. Press F1 to learn more about what Access can do for you.

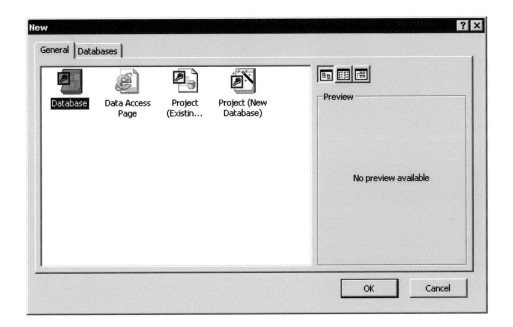

Organizing your life with Outlook

Microsoft Outlook (the senior version of Outlook Express) is the computer's version of your own personal organizer. It's an e-mail program, a diary, a scheduler, a reminder system, a contacts list, post-a-note scribble pad, and more, all in one program. And you can arrange the views and options to suit your own needs.

1. Click on **Start**, then **Programs**, then on **Microsoft Outlook** to open Outlook.
2. In the **Outlook Shortcuts** panel on the left of the main Outlook window, click on each item in turn to see what it offers.

3. Next, click on **View** on the Menu Bar and then on each of the menu options in turn, to see what the various views show.

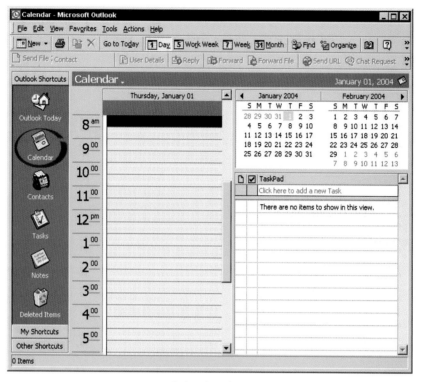

Calendar view

Some of the Accessories programs

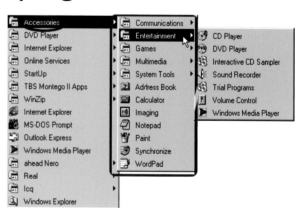

Click on **Start**, then **Programs**, then on **Accessories** to view the various applications available.

Here's an introduction to some of the more popular ones.

MAKING YOUR OWN RECORDINGS WITH SOUND RECORDER

This little program is used for making digital sound recordings if you have a computer microphone hooked up to your computer. It has the usual operating buttons for **Record**, **Play**, **Fast Forward**, and so on.

A click on the **Effects** menu option will allow you to change various properties, including adding echo. Similarly, clicking on the **Edit** button will open up more options for you to adjust.

 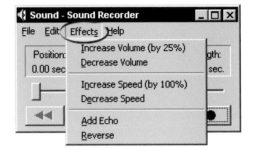

When you've finished making your recording, you can save it with a file name just like any other computer file so that you can play it, or send it to someone by e-mail.

NOTE:

Sound files are saved as a **.wav** file, and are rather large in size, so be careful not to clutter your system or other people's mailboxes with too many huge 'wave' files.

DOING CALCULATIONS WITH CALCULATOR

If you need to do a quick calculation, simply open the Calculator and start doing your calculations on your computer. There are two ways of entering the numbers onto the calculator's keypad:
- by clicking on each calculator button with your mouse, OR
- by using the number keys on your keyboard, and symbols such as **/** for dividing and ***** for multiplying.

A quick click on the **View** menu option will enable you to change your calculator from the standard model to a scientific calculator.

Standard calculator

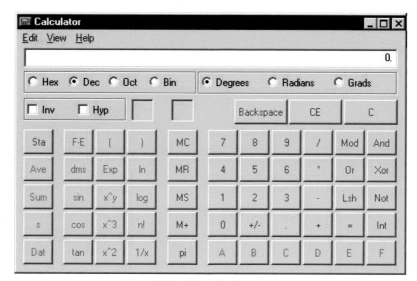

Scientific calculator

As usual, a quick press of the F1 button will open up the Calculator's Help menu.

A few other useful things to know

BACK UP YOUR DATA TO MINIMIZE THE RISK OF DATA LOSS
If you have many files saved on your computer, the last thing you want is to lose them all as a result of a computer 'crash' – where the hard drive becomes unusable and data gets corrupted – or program corruption. It is therefore **critically important** to save your important files to some other place so that if you do have hardware or software problems and you lose the data on your hard drive, you have another storage place with a back-up copy.

BACKING UP YOUR DATA REGULARLY

There are several ways in which you can keep a back-up of your important files, and different 'experts' will recommend different 'best' methods. Here are a few suggestions.

Saving to 3½-inch diskettes (not the best option)
If you don't have much data, you can save your files to floppy diskettes. These are the least stable form of disk to use as they are prone to failure, so it's a good idea to make two back-up copies in case one copy fails.

One disk holds only 1.44 megabytes, which is not much, so this is probably the least favoured method as you'll probably need to use many diskettes. Floppy diskettes are being phased out and many modern computers no longer include a floppy disk **[A:]** drive.

Saving to Rewritable Compact Disk (CD-RW) (a pretty good option)
This is similar to the previous option, but CDs have a capacity of around 700 megabytes, which is much greater than that of floppy diskettes. They are also far more stable. You'll need a CD Writer (not just a CD-ROM drive) installed on your computer, and you'll need to buy rewritable CDs that can be used over and over. This option has the convenience of portability, as you can use your files on another computer, such as a laptop, that has a CD Writer installed.

Saving to a second hard drive (a very good option)
If you can afford to have a second hard drive installed on your computer, this can be a better option than the first two methods. You simply save your work to the second hard drive, and if one of your drives fails, you can work on the second hard drive while the first one is being repaired, reformatted or replaced.

Making an automatic duplicate of your entire hard drive (an excellent option)
You can also buy hardware and software that can 'clone' your one drive and make an identical copy of it on your second hard drive – not just the data files, but all the installed programs and settings as well. Ask your technical advisor about having a 'RAID Controller' installed – which does this automatically all the time – or using software such as Symantec's Ghost program, which requires you to do the cloning regularly.

SAVING DATA MANUALLY TO ANOTHER DRIVE

Here's how to save data to a different drive (to a floppy disk on the **[A:]** drive, or to a CD on the **[D:]** drive or other drive, or to a second hard drive possibly named **[E:]** or **[F:]**.

1. If you're backing up to a removable disk, insert the floppy diskette or CD-RW disk into the correct disk drive port.
2. Open **Windows Explorer** and in the left-hand pane click on the ⊞ next to **My Computer** to open its contents and display all the drives. It should look similar to the illustration on the right.

3. Click on the folder you wish to back up (for example, My Documents) and **hold down** the mouse button to drag the folder.
4. Move the mouse button onto the drive (removable disk or second hard drive) until it is selected and highlighted.
5. Release the mouse button and the folder will be dropped into the destination drive. (This may take a few minutes, depending on how many files you are copying, and how large they are.)

NOTE:
If you drag a folder (or file) to a **different drive**, Windows will place a **copy** of it in the destination drive. If you drag-and-drop within the **same drive**, Windows will **remove** the item from the source folder and place it in the destination folder. Therefore, in the procedure above, your **My Documents** folder will stay intact in the **[C:]** drive, with a **copy** being placed in the destination drive.

SETTING YOUR COUNTRY'S DEFAULTS (DATE FORMAT, TIME ZONE, MEASUREMENTS, AND SO ON)

You can change several settings to make your computer suit the conventions of currency, date formats, and so on, for your country.

1. Click on **Start**, then on **Settings**, then **Control Panel**, then **double-click** on **Regional Settings** to open the **Regional Settings Properties** dialog box.
2. Click on each tab and use the ⏷ drop-down arrows to select the settings you require.
3. When you're done, click on **Apply**, then on **OK** to save the settings.

ADJUSTING THE VOLUME AND TONE ON YOUR SPEAKERS

1. **Right-click** on the little 🔊 speaker icon in the bottom right-hand section of the task bar.
2. Click on **Open Volume Controls**.

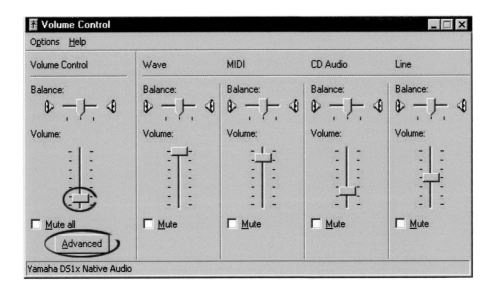

3. Click on the **Volume Control** sliding bar and hold down the mouse button as you move it up or down the slide to increase or decrease the volume.

4. If there is no **Advanced** button showing, click on **Options** and then on **Advanced Controls** so that it has a tick next to it.

5. Back in the main **Volume Control** dialog box click on **Advanced**.

6. Adjust the **Bass** and **Treble** as desired, sliding the little pointers left or right along the slide controls. (With some audio systems these options are greyed out because they are not available.)

7. Click on **Close**, then click on the ☒ button in the top right-hand corner of the **Volume Control** dialog box to close it.

NOTE:

You can adjust these controls again at any time.

TIP:

If you simply want to turn the volume up or down quickly, click once on the 🔊 **Volume** icon on the Taskbar and wait a second or two for the volume slide control to appear. Click and drag the slide control button up or down as necessary. To turn off the sound, click in the **Mute** check box.

The road ahead

As can be seen, personal computers have a lot to offer, and there are many ways of keeping abreast of what can be done and the ongoing enhancements constantly being offered by manufacturers of equipment, operating systems and applications. Here are some suggestions to help you on the road ahead.

HELP WITH THE WINDOWS 98 OPERATING SYSTEM

Here are two ways of getting more help with your Windows operating system. Try them now.

From the Start button:
1. Click on ![Start], then **Help**, and the **Windows Help** window will pop up.
2. Choose which tab view you want to use, and continue from there.

From the Desktop:
1. Click on any blank area on the **Desktop**, then press F1 , and the **Windows Help** window will pop up.
2. Choose an item from the **Contents** list, and continue from there.

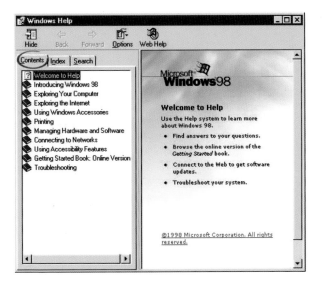

Finding help on a specific topic

Click on the **Index** tab and type a keyword for the topic you need help on, and Windows will list all items that relate to that keyword.

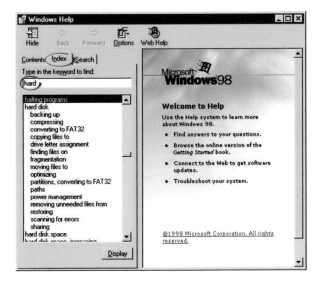

What version of windows do you have?

Note that the **Windows Help** window also tells you which version of **Windows** is installed on your computer. This is useful when you require technical support or want to install a new program that will be compatible with your operating system.

USE $F1$ IN ALL PROGRAMS

When working in a particular program, such as **Word** or **Internet Explorer**, you can also press $F1$ to call up the **Help** menu for that particular program.

MAKING USE OF INTERNET SEARCH ENGINES

Searching for information and help on the Internet is another very effective way of getting your questions answered. **Google** is an excellent search engine to use for this purpose.

MAKING USE OF THIS BOOK'S WEBSITE

Be sure to visit our Website at **www.reallyeasycomputerbooks.com** and browse around to check out our useful tips and links, and news of new books in this series of *Really, Really, Really Easy Computer Books*. There's also a bulletin board where you can ask questions for others to answer. Add this Website to your Favorites and visit periodically to get the latest updates.

CONTACTING THE AUTHORS

We've received wonderful feedback from users of Book 1 in this series, and the e-mails are still coming in. If you'd like to drop us a line to share your thoughts on Book 2, we'd love to hear from you. Contact us by e-mail via our Website at **www.reallyeasycomputerbooks.com**

Everything of the best!

Index